# ELEMENTARY MUSICIANSHIP

by
## Alvin Bauman
*Lecturer in Music*
*Columbia University*

1947
**PRENTICE-HALL, INC.**
*New York*

Dedicated to
THE MEMORY OF MY FATHER

# Preface

This text for beginning music courses is meant to be used as a manual. For the teacher it provides many examples, student drills, explanatory notes, and opportunity to expand both the material and its application. The book is designed not only to be read but to be written in, sung from, marked, annotated — to be used as each student's first reference work in treading the long path to expert musical craftsmanship and artistry. The text will, it is hoped, have meaning in terms of tonal experiences to be had far beyond the first music studies.

In using the text, two important principles should be kept in mind. First, theoretical knowledge is valid only if it supports tonal experience. The student must have ample opportunity to listen to and experience new musical phenomena before they are explained. Second, far more important than the subject matter is the work procedure. Through adequate methods of practice and approach to new problems the student will shape tools to help him in all his musical problems.

Teachers must insist that the student participate at the highest level of his artistry: He must sing as well as he can, he must not only attempt to produce pleasing tones but strive to express the emotional core of each melody. We, in our turn, have attempted to supply melodies of beauty from folk material and standard vocal and instrumental literature. The aesthetic experience must always parallel the technical growth.

The book is organized in twenty sections. The first term's work will, in general, carry through ten sections. The second term will continue to the end. Following the last section are canons, rounds, and two - and three-part compositions.

The main divisions of study are: Rhythms, sight singing, melodic and interval dictation, practice, theory, and analysis. Each section contains exercises and drills. Since the development of musical reflexes is not a matter of days or even weeks, many of the practice assignments will continue for some time. The exact time can be judged only on the basis of student performance. The teacher can readily expand or rearrange the sections to suit his plans and needs.

The material of this book has been gathered in the course of teaching classes in elementary musicianship. For enduring the test of my material and methods I owe thanks to a very generous student body. I am particularly grateful to Professor Douglas Moore, at whose suggestion this book was undertaken, and to Miriam Gideon, William J. Mitchell and Dr. Felix Salzer for their interest and advice. Finally, a very special thanks to my wife, Judith, for her help and understanding.

ALVIN BAUMAN

# Contents

VII

X CONTENTS

# Section 1.

### *Notes To The Teacher*

The teacher's first task in meeting a new class is to examine the students' musical possibilities. A test for aural accuracy should be the first musical activity of the first lesson. In a simple quick test the teacher plays unrelated tones on the piano; the students repeat each tone. After all the students have demonstrated their ability to reproduce a given tone, the teacher should play simple phrases, e.g.:

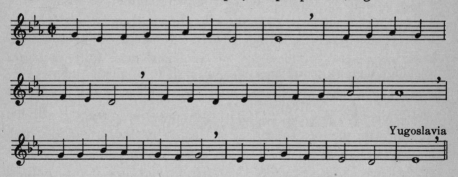

Yugoslavia

Students will repeat each phrase.

Finally, the class should memorize a melody. The one above will do. The recitation of the melody can wait until the second recitation hour or the end of the first hour. Another melody for memorization is:

Allegro moderato

Section 1 covers the following:

The twelve tones
　　Sharp, flat, and natural signs
Notation
　　Staff, clefs, and notes
Tonality
　　The concept of key center
　　The extension of one tone through the major triad and scales
　　The major scale
Rhythm
　　Beat, metre
　　Beat division in two and three parts
　　Notation of rhythm

The concepts of tonality and beat must be introduced through the students' experience and participation. They will understand tonality and rhythmic beat better if they can refer to their own physical sensations. Before each of these ideas is explained more fully, there are directions for student participation activities.

Rhythmic drills are accompanied by the students' beating with the heel of the foot. We suggest this as vastly superior to tapping with the hand or with the toe. The conscious element in flexing and extending the leg to establish the heel-beat leads to a greater physical awareness of rhythmic factors than do somewhat simpler and "more comfortable" methods.

The art of music involves the movement of sound in time. Sound elements consist mainly of tones. Tones are sounds of regular frequency, that is, of fixed pitch. A sound of fixed pitch comes from a church bell or a piano tone. The sound of a bass or snare drum or of almost any street noise is of variable frequency.

### The Twelve Tones

Music of Western civilization differentiates *twelve separate tones*. The twelve tones are each *repeated* at higher and lower levels. The distance from each tone to its nearest "repetition," above or below, is called an *octave*.

Each of the twelve tones is considered to be equidistant from each of its two neighboring tones. This distance is called a *half step* or a *half tone.* Two successive half steps make up the distance of a whole step or a whole tone.

The twelve tones are called:

A A-sharp BC C-sharp D D-sharp EF F-sharp G G-sharp

This is a continuous system, so that after G-sharp comes A, and so on through all the twelve tones. There are only seven letter names for twelve tones. Each tone, except B and E, is modified by the sharp. But each tone is an independent one. A and A-sharp are separate unrelated tones as are C and C-sharp, and so on. It is part of the musical tradition that only seven letter names are used.

## Sharp, flat, and natural signs

*Sharp* is represented by the sign #. The sharp sign indicates that the tone is one half step higher in pitch than the pitch name accompanying it. A# is one half tone higher than A. D# is one half tone higher than D.

A A#  BC C#  D D#  EF F#  G G#

These can also be named:

A B-flat BC D-flat D E-flat EF G-flat G A-flat

*Flat* is represented by the sign ♭. The flat sign indicates that the tone is one half step lower in pitch than the pitch name accompanying it. A♭ is one half step lower than A. E♭ is one half step lower than E.

A# can also be called B♭. A# and B♭ sound the same. C# and D♭ sound the same. Which other tones conform to this pattern?

# and ♭ are called *accidentals.*

The sign ♮ is called *natural* and means that there is no accidental affecting the tone. The signs #, ♭, and ♮ are all used to indicate higher or lower tones one half step away. In a composition, D♭ can be raised one half tone by the natural sign, D♮. C can be raised a half step by the sharp sign, C#. E can be lowered a half tone by the flat sign, E♭. G# can be lowered a half tone by the natural sign, G♮

Notice in the listing of the twelve tones that there are no accidentals between B and C, or between E and F. From B to C and from E to F are natural half steps.

### Drill

| | | |
|---|---|---|
| Sound B | : | sing an octave higher, an octave lower. |
| Sound C | : | sing an octave higher, an octave lower. |
| Sound A | : | sing a half step higher. What tone is this? |
| Sound F | : | sing a half step lower. What tone is this? |
| Sound E | : | sing an octave lower, then up a half step. |
| Sound A♭ | : | sing two half steps higher. |
| Sound G# | : | sing four half steps higher. What tone is this? |
| Sound B♭ | : | sing an octave higher, then two half steps down. |
| Sound C# | : | sing up the twelve half tones to C#, then back down to C#. |

### Notation

Tradition in all art depends very much on the ability to represent art compositions in permanent, communicable form. In music we attempt to represent composition by writing notes on music paper. We now use a system of notation that has been developed over many centuries. Our system of notation is based on the structure of the piano keyboard. There are only seven white notes between each octave, hence the seven letter names. The five tones accounted for by the accidentals match the five black keys in the octave. The two natural half steps, E—F, B—C, are not separated by black keys on the keyboard. Notation systems are always in the process of change in the pursuit of convenience and accuracy. Musical notation may look quite different in a hundred years.

### Staff, clefs, and notes

The fundamental of modern notation is the five-line staff.

The staff always appears with a clef sign. There are numerous clefs, of which we will use mainly two. One is called the G clef or *treble clef* and is represented by the sign:

The other is called the *F Clef* or *Bass Clef* and is represented by the sign:

There are other clefs in use, and we shall work with them. Two others are the *tenor clef*:

and the *alto clef*:

You may have guessed already the use of the clefs. Each covers a different range of tones. The clef names represent the range of voice parts, Treble, Alto, Tenor, and Bass. Different clef signs are used in vocal music to avoid the use of added lines above or below the staff. Amongst the orchestral instruments, the violin uses the treble clef, the viola uses the alto clef, the cello often uses the tenor clef as well as the bass clef. The treble and bass clefs (G and F) are often combined into one continuous system called the *great staff*. It is used in compositions for the piano.

The twelve tones in a range of about five octaves can be conveniently shown on the great staff. Tones are represented by notes on the staff placed on the lines or in the spaces.

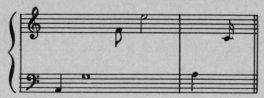

The first task we face in reading notes is to be able to identify the symbols on the staff. This is a mechanical process, the result of drill. As you work with music more, you will find that reading becomes a reflex, though now you will have to give it considerable thought.

These are the notes on the great staff:

*Note: the image below shows the great staff with notes labeled C A F B G D E*

### Drill

Make yourself seven cards each having a different note written on it.

Drill yourself with these cards until you can identify the notes in the proper lines and spaces. This drill will allow you to learn the position of each note on the staff irrespective of the relationship in distance between the notes. The note identification drill at the end of this section will increase your facility in reading notes in compositions.

### Tonality

Most music in the Western tradition is tonal music. This means that compositions are written in keys. It will be one of our important undertakings to hear, understand, and use the concept of tonality.

(*The teacher will play the following examples.* After each the students will sing the tone that comes first to mind.)

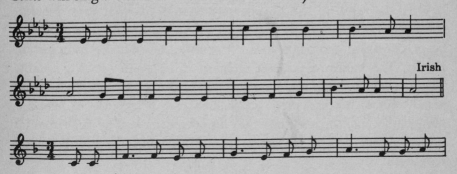

Irish

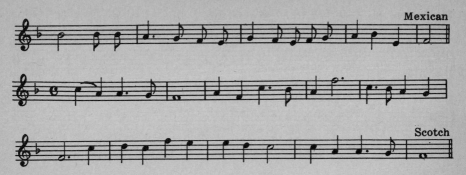

This tone is the "central" tone. It is called the *key tone*.

## The concept of key center

Tonal music, or music written in a key, is music that bases its tone structure on the dominance of one central tone from which the structure emanates and returns. In the examples above, the key tone of the first melody is A♭. You would object if after the first melody the tone B was sounded. In both the second and the third melodies the key tone is F. Each of the twelve tones may be used separately as a tonal center. Therefore, we say of a composition: "Nocturne in A" or "Scherzo in B♭."

## The extension of one tone through the major triad and scales

The simplest extension of a tonal center, other than the octave, is the *triad*. A triad can be sounded from every tone. For example,

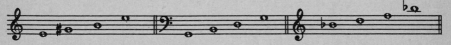

Sing triads from C, G, B♭, D, E, F#.

With the triad we still do not have enough material for a musical composition, because in the triad there is no movement. The triad can be played again and again in all its possibilities, but no composition results. The most we get is a series of calls, similar to bugle calls. These may be more or less pleasing, but, since all the tones of the triad blend with each other, there is no climax, no heightened or lessened tension, no conflict, and therefore no composition. The fundamental principle that creates movement is absent, namely, opposition and resolution.

The scale is a fundamental pattern that creates movement through the triad. There are many scales. A scale uses all or selected tones from the twelve tones in a continuous and generally a stepwise pattern ascending and descending.

The twelve-tone scale sounds:

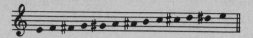

Without the twelve-tone scale the music of Wagner would be difficult to understand.

The whole-tone scale sounds:

Without the whole-tone scale the music of Debussy is hardly imaginable.

The five-tone scale sounds:

Without the five-tone scale we would be deprived of all the Irish reels.

### The major scale

The scale with which we shall begin work is the *major scale*. It sounds:

Sing the major scales from A, E, F#, B, D, Ab, C#, G.

The major scale uses only seven of the twelve tones. The distance between each of the tones will be either a half step or a whole step. The major scale on F:                 F major triad:

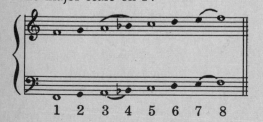

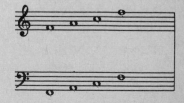

1  2  3  4  5  6  7  8

The 1st and 8th tones form an octave, i.e., a repetition. The distance between the 3rd and 4th tones is a half step. The distance between the 7th and 8th tones is a half step. All other adjacent tones are a whole step apart.

*The major scale is built of whole steps except between the 3rd and 4th degrees and between the 7th and 8th degrees.*

The C major scale:

1   2   3   4   5   6   7   8   7   6   5   4   3   2   1

The C major triad:

Each degree of the major scale has a different note name so that C and C# cannot be in the same scale. Every letter name must be included in the scale and each tone must be followed by a tone that uses the following letter name. Thus, the E major scale uses the letter names in order: E, F, G, A, B, C, D, E, with the appropriate accidentals.

### Drill

From B to C is a half step.                From E to F is _____step.
From B to C# is a whole step.              From E to F# is_____step.
From B♭ to C is a whole step.              From E♭ to F is_____step.

A half step above                          A half step below

      F  is _____.                                C is _____.

      B♭ is_____.                                D♭ is _____.

      C# is _____.                               A  is _____.

      D  is _____.                               F# is _____.

A half step above

     E is _____.

     G# is _____.

     A is _____.

A half step below

     Eb is _____.

     A# is _____.

     Gb is _____.

A whole step above

     Ab is _____.

     G is _____.

     Bb is _____.

     F# is _____.

     Eb is _____.

     A is _____.

     E is _____.

A whole step below

     Db is _____.

     A# is _____.

     F# is _____.

     F is _____.

     B is _____.

     C is _____.

     C# is _____.

Construct the F# major scale.

Notice that from the 6th degree, D#, there must be a whole step to the 7th degree. Will the 7th degree be F or E#?

E# sounds the same as F♮ .        B# sounds the same as C ♮ .

Fb sounds the same as E ♮ .        Cb sounds the same as B ♮ .

Construct the following major scales:

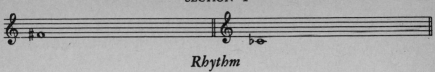

## Rhythm

*Teacher plays the examples on page 25. Students tap the heel of the foot with the music.*

Rhythm in music involves the manipulation of the time element to aid the tonal structure in the expression of a musical idea. It is a physical sensation of beat and pulse.

### Beat, metre

*Beat* is the measure of time. You have experienced this when you beat with the music. The conductor gives his beat with a baton.

Pulse is the continuing activity within the spaces marked off by the beats. It is the sensation of one beat flowing to the next, and may involve the use of many or few tones. The feeling of pulse is not unrelated to the sustained quality of a musical tone.

In the simplest rhythmic structures the beats recur regularly in the same patterns of stress and rest. When you tap your foot to music, some beats are stronger (harder), some are weaker (softer). These are called *accented* and *unaccented* beats.

*Metre* is the indication of a regular recurrence of a beat unit.
Metre of two is:        | |     | | |     | | |     |      etc.
Metre of three is:      | | | | | | | | | | | |     ·etc.

Each unit of two or three beats above is called a *measure* and is separated by bar lines. Within this outline of the regular beat occur many and varying rhythmic figures. These are arrived at by breaking down the beats into smaller units or combining beats into larger units. To indicate the division of measures we accent the first beat of each measure.

### Drill

(A) *Teacher sets a tempo for each of the metres of two, three, four, and five. The class beats each with the heel of the foot.* Keep the tempo steady!

(B) Now the class beats only the first beat of each measure within each of the metres.

(C) Finally, with each metre separately, the teacher claps or intones improvised rhythmic figures. The class, keeping the beat with the heel of the foot, repeats each figure.

### Beat division in two and three parts

Each beat of the measure is divided or combined in even and uneven parts to create rhythmic figures. The basic divisions of the beat are into two (2) and three (3) parts.

* Metre—2     |   |  |   |   |  |   |   |  |   |   |   ‖   *

2 part division    —.—.|   —.—.|   —.—.|  —.—.‖

3 part division    —..—..|  —..—..|  —..—..|  —..—..‖

Beat the metre as before, first on each beat, then only on the first beat of each measure. Intone the following beat divisions of two and three using the syllable "da" at a comfortable pitch.

### Drill

2 metre   |    |    |    |    |    |    |    |    |    |    |  ‖

A.   —. —.. | —. —. | —.. —.. | —. —..‖

B.   —.. —.. | —.. —. | —.. —.. | —. —. ‖

C.   —.. —. | —.. —. | —. —. | —. —.. ‖

D.   —. —. | —.. —. | —. —. | —. —. ‖

E.   —. —.. | —. —.. | —. —.. | —. —.. ‖

F.   —. —. | —.. —.. | —. —. | —.. —.. ‖

G.   —.. —. | —. —. | —.. —.. | —. —. ‖

H.   —. —.. | —. —.. | —. —. | —. —. ‖

I.   —.. —.. | —. —. | —.. —. | —. —. ‖

J.   —. —. | —.. —.. | —. —. | —.. —.. ‖

### Notation of rhythm

The length of tones in rhythmic figures is indicated by the heads, stems, and flags on the notes.

---

*The double bar line is a traditional sign indicating the end.

All rhythmic patterns arise from further subdividing the beat or combining the parts in patterns.

| NOTES | | RESTS |
|---|---|---|
| o | whole | — |
| ♩ | half | – |
| ♩ | quarter | ⸯ |
| ♪ | eighth | ⁊ |
| ♪ | sixteenth | ⁊ |
| ♪ | thirty-second | ⁊ |

Notice that the notes and rests have no absolute value. Their value is only proportionate one to the other.

These note units are combined within the metre given at the beginning of every composition. We must be told which of these notes is the unit of measurement for each beat. Does ♩ make one beat? Does ♩ make one beat? To answer the question, before each composition there are two numbers in a fraction, e.g., $\frac{3}{4}$. The numerator indicates the recurring outline, in this case 3 ( | | | ) , and the lower number indicates the unit of measurement, in this case a quarter note ♩. In the metre $\frac{3}{4}$ no measure will exceed the value of three quarter notes. There are three beats to each measure; the quarter note is valued at one beat.

Let us see now how the division of beats looks with the note figures.

Since only two eighth notes ♫ equal a quarter ♩, we place a 3 over the notes to show a three-part division of the beat. The 3 indicates that we wish the three eighth notes to equal in value one quarter note. This is called a *triplet*.

### Drill

Write out the drill on page 12 showing the beat divisions of two and three. Use standard metre sign and notes.

A ♫ ♫♩ |
B
C
D
E
F
G
H
I
J

Bar the following rhythmic figures.

Write four measures in each of the following metres using as many different note and rest values as you can.

3/8
2/8
4/4
5/4
6/8

*Drill*: *note identification*

Turn to any page with melodies. Beat a two metre with the heel of the foot. On each beat read aloud the name of each successive note, beginning with the first melody. Do this at a slow and even tempo. Then increase the speed. *Set the tempo before you begin!*

Continuing the metrical beat read aloud the first note in each measure.

Finally, still with the metrical beat, read aloud the first and last notes on each line. You will find with this exercise that you will be looking ahead, that is, reading one note while you look at the next.

# Section 2.

Class work in Section 2 should begin with the note identification drill that appears as the last drill of Section 1.

Emphasis should be placed on the daily practice of scale drills.

In the scale exercises in rhythmic patterns we suggest that the teacher demonstrate the parts marked *. Only when a new type of exercise is first used will demonstrations be called for.

The sight singing melodies will include some elements not yet explained, e.g., simple examples of the use of the dot. The teacher will demonstrate the effect of the dot in lengthening the note value of a sustained tone, but the explanation and drills will come in the next section.

## Rhythm

You now know what metre is, what a measure is, and you can identify the different rest and note values. Your control over rhythmic elements will come by practice.

### Patterns to be intoned

Each lesson will contain rhythmic patterns in different metres to be intoned. Beat the metre with the heel of the foot. Begin by beating each beat of the measure. Then beat only the first count of each measure. Intone the patterns using the syllable "da" at a comfortable pitch. Every note must be sounded its full length; every rest must be "unsounded."

Intone the following rhythmic patterns:

Transcribe the patterns above into $\frac{2}{8}$ metre; into $\frac{2}{2}$ metre.

## Scales

Visualize (in the "mind's eye") the scale of A major as it is written on paper. Sound A on the piano; sing the scale naming the notes. It is not necessary to say the accidental. It is too awkward to sing the words "C-sharp." But sing the correct tone. For the tones A and A♭ you will use the name "A", but you will sing A♭ a half tone lower than A ♮. How many accidentals are in the key of A major? Name them in order as they appear going up the scale.

Visualize the scale of B♭ major. Sing it. What are the accidentals? Do the same for the major scales of G, E, A♭, D.

### Signatures of major keys

We say of each key that it has its own signature. The signature of a key includes all the accidentals used in the scale. Traditionally, a tonal composition is preceded by its key signature to inform the reader what accidentals are used regularly throughout the composition.

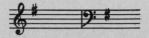

means that the composition uses F# regularly. The key is G major.

F major:                                     A major:

The signatures of the major scales are as follows:

SCALE        ACCIDENTALS

| SCALE | ACCIDENTALS |
|---|---|
| C | |
| G | F$\sharp$ |
| D | F$\sharp$C$\sharp$ |
| A | F$\sharp$C$\sharp$G$\sharp$ |
| E | F$\sharp$C$\sharp$G$\sharp$D$\sharp$ |
| B | F$\sharp$C$\sharp$G$\sharp$D$\sharp$A$\sharp$ |
| F$\sharp$ | F$\sharp$C$\sharp$G$\sharp$D$\sharp$A$\sharp$E$\sharp$ |
| F | B$\flat$ |
| B$\flat$ | B$\flat$E$\flat$ |
| E$\flat$ | B$\flat$E$\flat$A$\flat$ |
| A$\flat$ | B$\flat$E$\flat$A$\flat$D$\flat$ |
| D$\flat$ | B$\flat$E$\flat$A$\flat$D$\flat$G$\flat$ |
| G$\flat$ | B$\flat$E$\flat$A$\flat$D$\flat$G$\flat$C$\flat$ |

Knowledge of the signatures is a convenience. Measured in time saved you will consider it indispensable. Memorize the signatures the same way you memorized the note names. Make a separate card for each signature and drill.

The following drill should be used as a daily exercise until you can perform it without hesitation. At that point you will have gained almost all it has to offer because you will be singing it automatically, without thought. It will then be relegated to the store of knowledge that can be used with minimum effort.

### Drill

Practice the following scale drill in *all* major keys using both treble and bass clefs. Write them in your notebook.

## The Slur

The sign ⌢ or ⌣ is called a *slur* or phrase mark. It indicates that the group of notes outlined by the sign is to be considered a separate group from the preceding and following groups. Since the rhythm must be continuous we give only a slight accent to the first note of the group. < or > is an accent mark.

When ⌢ or ⌣ joins successive tones of the same pitch it is a tie and means that the time value of the sustained tone is equal to the addition of the values of all the tied notes. For example: 𝅗𝅥 𝅗𝅥 𝅘𝅥 would indicate that the tone is held for five beats in any of the above metres.

When ⌢ includes two or more notes of a song, it may mean that the tones are sung on one syllable.

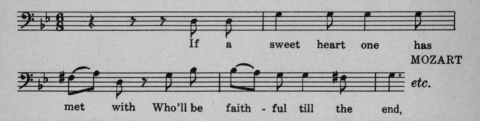

If      a      sweet  heart  one      has

MOZART

met   with   Who'll be   faith - ful   till   the      end,

Also practice the exercises as follows:

All drills moving up the scale must also be practiced going downward.

## Scales in rhythmic patterns

Sing the following scale exercises in rhythmic patterns. Establish the key and the tempo. Beat two measures before you begin to sing. Keep the beat strictly and sing through all the exercises in the same key. Then begin in the same way with the exercises in the next key. Sing the names of the tones and/or the syllable "loo." Try beating only the first beat of each measure.

*These patterns are to be demonstrated by the teacher.

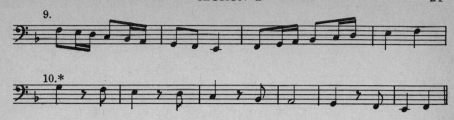

## For the student:

(3)  measure 1. [notation] Four tones in one beat. Each note is
a_____.

(5)  measure 1. [notation] | The second beat is a_____rest.

(7)  measure 1. [notation] |Only the first half of the beat is sounded.
is a_____rest.

(8)  measure 3.   [notation]   The second beat is divided in two. The
first half consists of a_____note.
The second half consists of two
_____notes. Write this measure
in $\frac{2}{2}$ metre.

(10) measure 1.   [notation]   The second beat is divided in two.
Only the last part of the beat
sounds. The second beat consists
of a_____rest and a_____note.

### Dictation

These scale patterns will now be dictated in the keys of G major
and Eb major. What are the signatures?

### Procedure for dictation

(1)  The key tone and scale will be played.

(2)  The melody or scale pattern will be played twice.

(3)  Think through the melody or scale pattern once.

(4)  It will be played once more.

(5)  Think through the melody five or six or more times in the
original tempo until it is so well memorized that you can think it
through at a much slower tempo.

(6)  Re-establish the key tone and scale in your mind.

(7)  Write the dictated melody or scale pattern.

Postpone the writing of the dictation until you have completely mem-

---

*These patterns are to be demonstrated by the teacher.

orized it. The slower you approach the paper, the faster you will write
the correct dictation. Memorize and then "slow down" the melody.

### The Movement of Scale Degrees

We spoke of the scale as the simplest structure creating movement
through the triad. Each tone of the scale has a different function in
this movement. The key tone is at once the source of movement and
the end to which it returns. The key tone is also called the *tonic*. The
tonic is the most stable note of the key. It defines the key. In the
sound of the tonic there is no necessity for further action. The keynote
is a sound of rest or stability.

The tones of stability in the scale are the 1st, 3rd, 5th, and octave;
these comprise the *tonic triad,* sometimes called the I chord.

Sing or play the scale ascending up to the 7th degree. Are you
content to end there? or do you feel that the octave, the key tone must
follow? The 7th degree of the scale is called the *leading tone;* it resolves to the tonic. There is a real tension in the sound of the 7th
degree of the major scale. The resolution to the tonic is inevitable
and completes the movement of the leading tone.

The other tones, the 2d, 4th, 6th degrees, of the scale tend to
move to the rest tones. The more active tones create motion in music
by their inherent need to proceed to rest tones. They are never "re-
quired" to resolve in a particular way, though the nearest resolutions
are the adjacent tones.

Our task is to get the "feel" of each major scale degree by relating
each active tone to a rest tone. The tonic, the leading tone, the 2d
degree, and so forth—each arouses a different physical sensation. It
will be necessary to "feel" the sensations of each tone many times
before you will develop an immediate response to each of the scale
degrees. If we succeed with the major scale degrees, all the other scales
will be easier.

The first step is to *think* everything before you sing. Do as little
mechanically as possible. In other words, learn everything consciously
so that you can recall it and work with it.

The next steps will be sight singing, dictation, and practice. The
most important principle for your work is: *Use what you already know
to solve new problems.*

Example:

lish a very slow tempo so that without changing the tempo you
erform this measure as follows:

tones without stems fill in the scale passages within the skips.
ese *sotto voce* (in an undertone, subdued) in contrast to the
l melody, which is sung in full voice. The major scale is your
g tool.
re there are difficult skips that need more work, label above
te the scale degree it represents.

u learn the sound of the leap from the 3rd to the 6th degree
r vocabulary will have been increased by one important tone com-
ation. This vocabulary should increase by approximately thirty new
ombinations a week.

## Tempo and Expression Markings

Often the composer gives us not only the tones and the rhythm but
also written indications of the results he desires to accomplish. These
written directions occur throughout the composition, and are called
*markings*.

At the beginning of a composition the composer may indicate whether
the ensuing work is to be done slowly, or slowly but not too slowly, or
fast, and so forth. Or the composer may dictate the general mood of
the composition. The expressions that are used are traditional. You
will have to acquaint yourself with them through a dictionary of musical
terms. Sometimes the composer's instructions are so exact as to give

### Dictation practice

*The teacher will play* C. Think silently the C major scale up a
down an octave. Now write the notes that the teacher plays. Meas
each tone from C through the major scale.

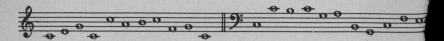

Now in the key of E♭ major. What is the signature?

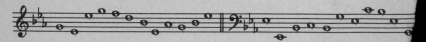

Now in the key of B major. What is the signature?

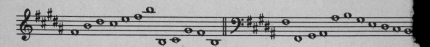

Correct your dictation by writing in the correct notes over the
you have already written. *Don't* change your first markings. You
be able to see where your difficulties lie and you will be able to g
yourself in your home drill.

### Sight Singing Procedure

(1) Look through the melody.

(2) Find the key and the metre.

(3) Establish the tonic pitch. If you don't have a piano, use any comfortable pitch, but think the correct key.

(4) Sing the scale.

(5) Establish a slow even tempo. Beat at least two measures before
you sing. The tempo should be slow enough for you to sing through
the melody without stopping the beat. *You must look ahead.* A slow
tempo will allow you to do this.

(6) Now, sing through the melody from beginning to end.

Circle the difficult places; these are your practice points. If there
are skips or leaps, that is, movements from one tone to another two
or more steps away, sing through the scale in between.

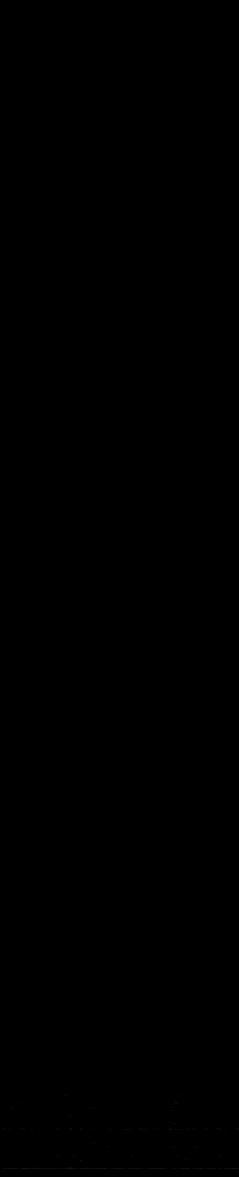

Example:

Establish a very slow tempo so that without changing the tempo you can perform this measure as follows:

The tones without stems fill in the scale passages within the skips. Sing these *sotto voce* (in an undertone, subdued) in contrast to the original melody, which is sung in full voice. The major scale is your working tool.

Where there are difficult skips that need more work, label above each note the scale degree it represents.

If you learn the sound of the leap from the 3rd to the 6th degree your vocabulary will have been increased by one important tone combination. This vocabulary should increase by approximately thirty new combinations a week.

## Tempo and Expression Markings

Often the composer gives us not only the tones and the rhythm but also written indications of the results he desires to accomplish. These written directions occur throughout the composition, and are called *markings*.

At the beginning of a composition the composer may indicate whether the ensuing work is to be done slowly, or slowly but not too slowly, or fast, and so forth. Or the composer may dictate the general mood of the composition. The expressions that are used are traditional. You will have to acquaint yourself with them through a dictionary of musical terms. Sometimes the composer's instructions are so exact as to give

### Dictation practice

*The teacher will play* C. Think silently the C major scale up and down an octave. Now write the notes that the teacher plays. Measure each tone from C through the major scale.

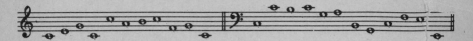

Now in the key of E♭ major. What is the signature?

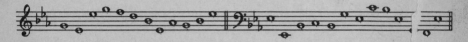

Now in the key of B major. What is the signature?

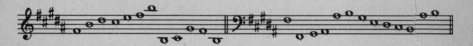

Correct your dictation by writing in the correct notes over the ones you have already written. *Don't* change your first markings. You will be able to see where your difficulties lie and you will be able to guide yourself in your home drill.

### Sight Singing Procedure

(1) Look through the melody.

(2) Find the key and the metre.

(3) Establish the tonic pitch. If you don't have a piano, use any comfortable pitch, but think the correct key.

(4) Sing the scale.

(5) Establish a slow even tempo. Beat at least two measures before you sing. The tempo should be slow enough for you to sing through the melody without stopping the beat. *You must look ahead.* A slow tempo will allow you to do this.

(6) Now, sing through the melody from beginning to end.

Circle the difficult places; these are your practice points. If there are skips or leaps, that is, movements from one tone to another two or more steps away, sing through the scale in between.

a metronome number indicating the precise number of beats per minute.

♩ = 80 means that the proportion of eighty quarter notes per minute is the exact tempo.

Within the composition there may be further directions. For example, *p*·means piano, soft; *f* means forte, loud;  <  indicates an increase in volume, and so on.

Tempo and expression markings will help you to grasp the composer's conceptions. Whenever you meet an unfamiliar term, look it up in a dictionary of musical terms.

### *Sight Singing—Melodies*

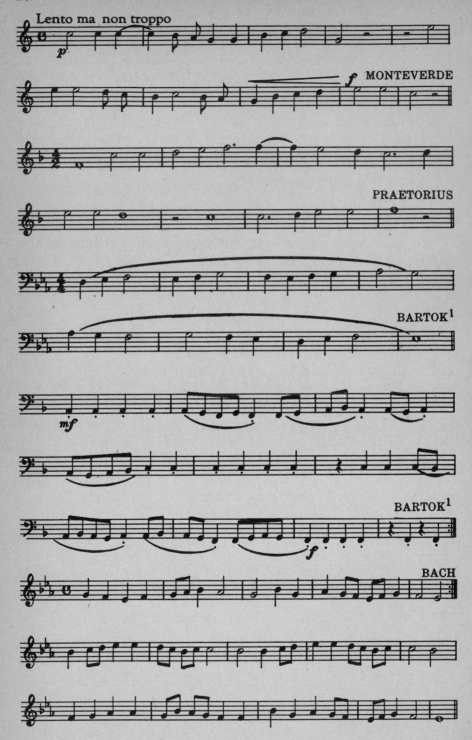

Hungarian Dance BARTOK[1]

MOZART

## Practice Suggestions

The following procedure has been found to be most productive in learning new sound combinations.

Write and work with two major scales each day, so that all twelve major scales are covered each week.

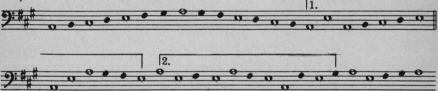

and

Establish the key and sing the scale. Then, in a slow tempo, beginning with the tonic (later on with any tone) sing up and down in scales and leaps concentrating on problems taken from the sight singing melodies. These exercises cannot be given to you; they can result only from your own creative practice. At least ten minutes each day should be used in this way. The beginning of this type of exercise might one day "look" as follows.

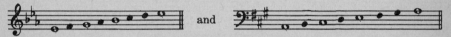

Notice that we approach all problems *ascending* and *descending*. The skip

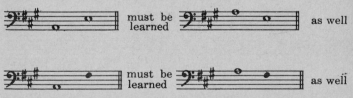

must be learned

as well

must be learned

as well

1 Reprinted by permission of Boosey & Hawkes, Inc., New York, New York.

# Section 3.

===============================

## Notes To The Teacher

Section 3 covers the following:

Rhythm
    The function of the dot
    Patterns to be intoned
    The up-beat
    Scale patterns
Practice
Principal and dependent tones
Passing tones
Neighboring tones
Sight singing: melodies

The identification of principal, dependent, passing, and neighboring tones is an elementary step in the analysis of musical motion. Analysis will be continued and intensified until the end of the year's work.

## Rhythm

There are two ways of extending the rhythmic value of a sustained tone; by the use of a tie ( ⌢ ) or a dot.

The tie connecting adjacent tones of the same pitch sustains the rhythmic value of the tone by the value of all the tied notes. For example, in $\frac{4}{4}$ metre the pattern ♩‿♩ indicates a sustained tone of three beats; ♩‿♩ indicates six beats; ♩‿♩♩ indicates four beats.

## The function of the dot

The dot lengthens a tone by one half (½) its own value.

In $\frac{2}{4}$ metre

$\half$ = 2 beats

$\half\,\half$ = 3 beats

$\half.$ = 3 beats

The dot lengthens $\half$ by the value of $\quarter$

$\quarter$ $\eighth$ $\eighth$

can be written

$\quarter.$ $\eighth$

The dot lengthens $\quarter$ by the value of $\eighth$

A dot may accompany a rest as well as a note.

Intone the following patterns:

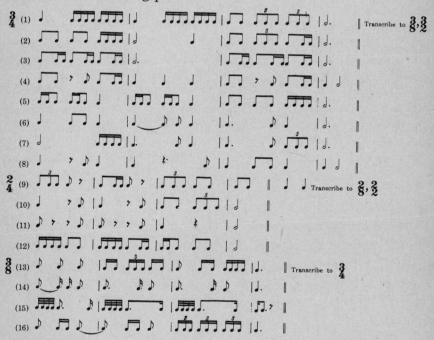

# The up-beat

Not all melodies begin on the first beat of the first measure, the traditional down-beat of the conductor's baton. Many melodies begin with incomplete measures, one or two beats before the first complete measure. This is called *anacrusis* or *up-beat*. It gives a sense of rhythmic anticipation, setting up a rhythmic and often a tonal conflict that drives the musical momentum from the start.

Such a melody is "Hallelujah, Bum Again."

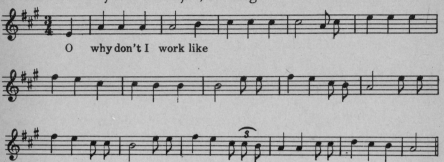

O    why don't I  work like

Notice the last measure of the melody. It is also incomplete with only a 𝅘𝅥 . Both the incomplete measures at the beginning and end of a composition using the up-beat must total one complete measure. Thus, in the melody above, the 𝅘𝅥 at the beginning and the 𝅗𝅥 at the end complete three full beats in $\frac{3}{4}$ metre.

Do you get the sense of anticipation in singing from the up-beat to the first beat of the measure? The strong tonal value of the A (in A major) plus its position as the strong beat of the first measure supports the feeling that E (up-beat) is introductory. The words of the song lend further support. Often in performing this song the up-beat is sustained to intensify the anticipation before beginning the rollicking rhythm.

Sing the following scale patterns:

These will now be dictated in the keys of C major and A major.

## Practice

In Section 2 you were given exercises to sing using $\frac{3}{4}$, $\frac{4}{4}$, and $\frac{4}{5}$ metres in continuous scale patterns ascending and descending. These must be continued every day in all keys. In the next section this exercise will be extended.

Also continue to work on new tone combinations in attempting to increase your vocabulary of sound, and to get the "feel" of each scale degree. Try the following pattern.

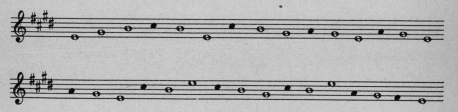

## Principal and Dependent Tones

We defined the art of music as the movement of sound in time. You have already manipulated elements of this movement.

In speaking of the major scale we said it moved from one tone to the octave above or below. And within the major scale each tone serves a function in the movement. There are the more active tones, the 2d, 4th, 6th, and 7th degrees and the more stable tones, the 1st, 3rd, 5th, and octave. The most important tone is the tonic. It generates the scale which moves stepwise from one tone of the triad to the next until the octave is complete. We call the 1st, 3rd, and 5th tones (tonic triad) *principal tones*.

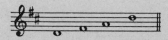

The 2d, 4th, 6th, and 7th degrees connect these tones. They are called *dependent tones.*

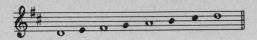

Dependent tones connect or move between principal tones. The dependent tones are carriers of the movement to the more stable points which outline the movement.

There are principal (P) and dependent (D) tones in melodies also. Since a melody is not a predictable pattern like the scale, we distinguish between principal and dependent elements by listening for the relative activity or stability. A composition moves from one point of rest to another. And in between are the carriers of the motion, the active dependent tones.

### Passing Tones

Dependent tones may be passing tones. The 2d, 4th, 6th, and 7th degrees of the scales are passing tones, that is, the scale movement goes through the passing tones to the tones of the triad. In the melody, "Three Blind Mice":

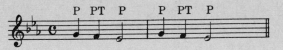

G is a principal tone.

F is a passing tone.

Eb is a principal tone.

G passes through F to Eb.

A passing tone is necessarily part of a group of at least three tones, each a step from the next. Passing tones can never be leaps, since in leaps we outline a space but do not connect or pass through a space.

From D to G is a leap of a fifth.

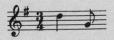

From G stepwise back to D

G is a principal tone. D is a principal tone. ABC are passing tones moving from G to D.

On pages 33-36, label the passing tones "PT" and the principal tones "P."

## Neighboring Tones

Now look at the following figure.

Both the first and the second E are principal tones. What is D? It does not move away from the E to another tone. No motion goes through it. The melody moves back to E. D is called a *neighboring tone*. A tone may be accompanied by a neighbor above or below—upper neighboring tones and lower neighboring tones.

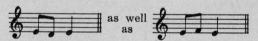

Label all the neighboring tones "N" in the melodies on pages 33-36.

Now we can identify the principal tones (P), the passing tones (PT), and the neighboring tones (N). There will be other dependent tones that are neither passing tones nor neighbors. Label these dependent tones "D."

## Sight Singing — Melodies

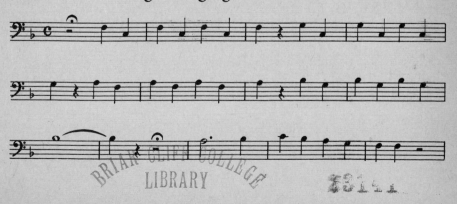

MOZART

Slowly    BRAHMS

BARTOK[1]

BACH

MOZART

U.S.

BRAHMS

1 Reprinted by permission of Boosey & Hawkes, Inc., New York, New York

BARTOK[1]

U.S.

MOZART

BACH

English Carol

U.S.

Con spirito

1 Reprinted by permission of Boosey & Hawkes, Inc., New York, New York.

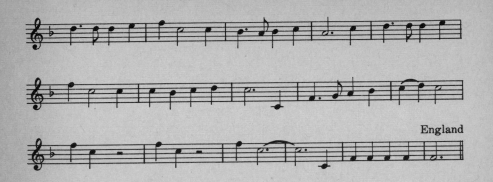

England

# Section 4.

## *Notes To The Teacher*

Section 4 covers the following:

Rhythm
    Six, nine, twelve metres; the dotted quarter as the unit beat
    Patterns to be intoned
    Scales in rhythmic patterns
Minor scales
    Minor signatures
Signatures
Sight singing
    Melodies
Dictation
Practice

Though the student is not yet completely at ease with the major scale, we begin now with the minor scales, primarily because the student will be hearing minor as well as major music in his listening. We also find that, if the treatment of the minor scale is postponed until the major is completely learned, the change is needlessly difficult for the student.

In this section we introduce a type of scansion for each melody, in labeling scale passages, neighboring and passing tones. The result of this procedure is that the student sees structural groups within the melody rather than single tones.

Also introduced in this section is dictation of four-note groups from major scales, e.g.,

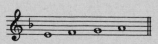

the 3rd, 4th, 5th, and 6th degrees in C major. Any group like this can be identified with either of two scales. At this point the student need identify only the scale degrees of one possibility. The student continues the scale pattern until he reaches the tonic, and figures out the number of the scale degrees from the tonic.

## Rhythm

You have worked thus far with metres of two and three. Within these metrical units various combinations of rhythmic elements have been used, all based on the beat division of two or three parts.

The metres of two and three are the fundamentals of all metrical units. They are called *simple* metres. When we go above three to the metres of four, five, six, eight, and so on, we deal with *compound* metres. A compound metre results from combining simple metres. Thus, four is the resultant of two plus two; five of two plus three or three plus two, and so forth.

### Six, nine, twelve metres; the dotted quarter as the unit beat

In the exercises thus far the normal beat division has been in two parts; ♩ = ♫ Whenever the division of three was used the triplet sign was marked above the notes. Certain metres use the three-part beat division regularly, as the normal division. These metres are six, nine, twelve.

The six metre is a compound of two. Each beat has three parts. In $\frac{6}{8}$ for example, the unit of measurement is

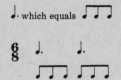

The measure is performed as a two metre, with two beats. The result of an equal three-part division of the beat makes for six eighth notes.

Nine metre is considered to be a compound three. In $\frac{9}{8}$ each ♩. is one beat.

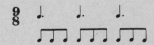

Twelve metre is considered to be a compound four.

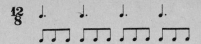

You see that each beat is represented by ♩. , and there is no need for the triplet sign since ♫ equals ♩. . On the other hand if we use two ♪ to ♩. it must be marked ♫̄² , and similarly with four ♬̄⁴ These are called *duolet* and *quartolet*.

Intone the following rhythmic patterns:

**4/4** (1) [rhythmic notation] ‖Transcribe to **4/8**

(2) [rhythmic notation] ‖

(3) [rhythmic notation] ‖

(4) [rhythmic notation] ‖

(5) [rhythmic notation] ‖

(6) [rhythmic notation] ‖

(7) [rhythmic notation] ‖

(8) [rhythmic notation] ‖

**6/8** (9) [rhythmic notation] ‖Transcribe to **6/4**

(10) [rhythmic notation] ‖

(11) [rhythmic notation] ‖

(12) [rhythmic notation] ‖

(13) [rhythmic notation] ‖

**3/8** (14) [rhythmic notation] ‖ Transcribe to **3/4**

(15) [rhythmic notation] ‖

(16) [rhythmic notation] ‖

(17) [rhythmic notation] ‖

(18) [rhythmic notation] ‖

(19) [rhythmic notation] ‖

* The figure ♩.♪ has been presented in previous work. This is the first time it is given on one beat; before it included two beats in 3/8 metre. No matter what the metre, the pattern will sound the same. Because students are sometimes inaccurate in performing ♪♩ on one beat we shall explain it here.

**2/4** ♩ ♩ | ♩ ♩

♩ = ♬

The pattern ♩.♪ sounds the first and the last tones of ♬ . The pattern may be varied and appear ♪𝄾♩ , that is, the eighth note is not sustained by a dot ♪ .

Sing the following scale patterns.

These will now be dictated in E♭ and A major.

### Minor Scales

In our discussion of tonality in Section 1 we mentioned many scales, of which the major was one. We now proceed to the minor scale, which, with the major scale gives us a grasp of the tonalities most used in Western music of the seventeenth, eighteenth, and nineteenth centuries.

The minor scale sounds:

Sing the minor scales from C, F, B♭, D, F♯.

The minor scale, like the major, is a seven-tone scale. There are half steps between the 2d and 3rd degrees and between the 5th and 6th degrees.

---

The third ♪ of the ♫♫ is omitted. The usual difficulty with the performance of ♫ is the tendency to perform it ♪³♪ , as a triplet figure. One way to overcome this inaccuracy is to think the pattern thus: ♪♪ ♪♪ ♫. ♫. that is, think of ♪ as belonging to the following note. In ⅜ the figure ♫ is parallel with ♫ in ¾.

G minor scale:                                    G minor triad:

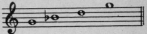

## Dictation

Identify the following triads as major or minor. Think each one through before writing.

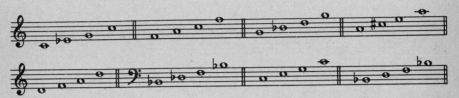

F minor scale:                                    F minor triad:

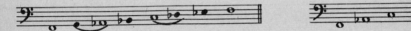

Notice the position of the half steps.

*Write* the following minor scales:

## Minor signatures

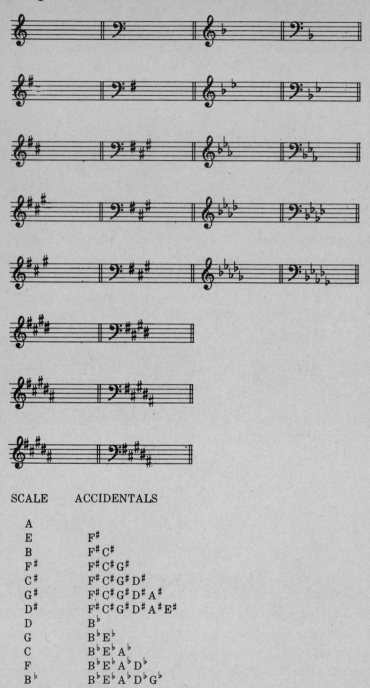

SCALE    ACCIDENTALS

A
E        F♯
B        F♯ C♯
F♯       F♯ C♯ G♯
C♯       F♯ C♯ G♯ D♯
G♯       F♯ C♯ G♯ D♯ A♯
D♯       F♯ C♯ G♯ D♯ A♯ E♯
D        B♭
G        B♭ E♭
C        B♭ E♭ A♭
F        B♭ E♭ A♭ D♭
B♭       B♭ E♭ A♭ D♭ G♭

The minor scales we have explained are called the *natural* minor scales and govern the signatures of the minor keys. Actually, we rarely find the minor scale used in compositions in this form. Generally an alteration is made on the 6th and/or the 7th degrees to accelerate the movement to the tonic. The alterations come from the major scale. For example:

uses A ♮ and B ♮ from the C major scale. When these alterations occur, the scale is called a *mixed* scale, that is, it has elements of major and minor.

How can one tell if a scale is a mixed major scale or a mixed minor scale? This is judged by the sound of the 3rd degree of the scale. If the 3rd degree sounds major, the scale is major; if the 3rd sounds minor, the scale is minor. The fundamental element distinguishing major and minor is the sound of each triad.

The triad of C minor:                           The triad of C major:

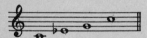                            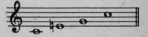

All the tones are the same except the third degree of the scale: E ♮ in major; E♭ in minor. The triad as the structural outline of the scale also defines the difference between major and minor.

D major mixed:                                  D minor mixed:

                            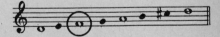

### Signatures

We now know of two sets of signatures, major and minor. How can one tell if the signature represents major or minor? The final deciding factor as always will be the sound of the music. You will have to read through the melody to decide whether it is major or minor.

Signatures must actually be viewed as directives to the reader telling him which accidentals are regularly used. Often we find only partial signatures.

This melody is based on the key tone F; the tonality F minor. Any automatic decision about the key based upon the traditional signature of three flats, i.e., E♭ major or C minor, would be incorrect. It will always be necessary to hear the melody to decide on the key tone and the tonality. This will require a careful observation of the accidentals and an increasing skill in manipulating whole steps and half steps.

### Sight Singing

In all the following melodies mark the scale passages, passing tones, and neighboring tones. Where there are leaps that you find difficult, mark the scale degree above the tones.

Scale passage:
Passing tone: PT
Neighboring tone: N

## *Sight singing—melodies*

1 Reprinted by permission of Boosey & Hawkes, Inc., New York, New York.

MOZART

BARTOK[1]

U.S.

U.S.

BACH

BACH

Moderato

ROSSINI

1 Reprinted by permission of Boosey & Hawkes, Inc., New York, New York.

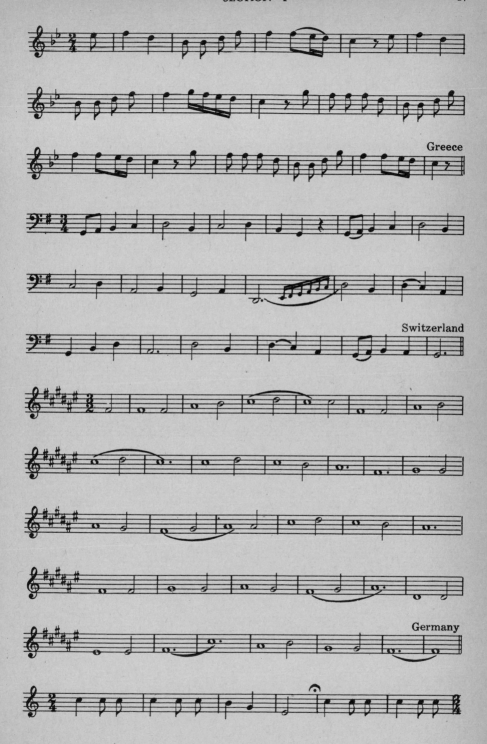

Greece

Switzerland

Germany

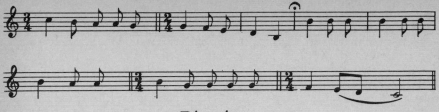

## Dictation

The following four-note groups from major scales will be played. You will identify the scale degrees. For example:

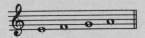

is, in C major, the 3rd, 4th, 5th, and 6th degrees. In F major these tones are the 7th, 1st, 2d, and 3rd degrees. You will think through the pattern and continue up or down the scale until you reach what feels like the tonic. From this you will decide which scale degrees are represented.

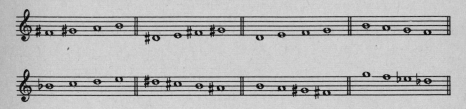

## Practice

You have been singing the major scales in patterns as follows:

Now add the remaining three patterns to this series.

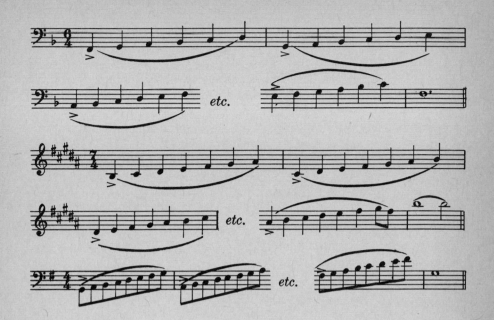

# Section 5.

Section 5 covers the following:

Rhythmic patterns to be intoned
Measurement of distance—intervals
Sight singing: melodies
Practice
Dictation
  Tone groups from major scales
  Melodies

Sections 5 and 6 are considered drill sections. We mean that all the material in these two sections shall be prepared, drilled, and recited in class. This is to give the teacher an adequate gauge of the class progress as well as to solidify and reinforce the knowledge and especially the practice procedures already explained.

*Measurement of distance — intervals.* The student is actually not ready to hear and work with all the intervals. The dictation of intervals and concentration of work on intervals will begin in Section 11. We introduce the mechanical measurement of intervals at this point because (1) the teacher must often talk about intervals in correcting the sight singing, and (2) the student, at this point, often fails to see the far-reaching importance of his study of scales. The discussion and mechanical measurement of intervals gives the student a fleeting but impressive glimpse of the future use of his scale knowledge while he gains experience with musical terminology.

*Dictation.* We now drop the singing and dictation of scales in rhythmic patterns to begin the dictation of melodies. The dictation procedure outlined in Section 2 should be followed exactly. The student *must* memorize before writing. Dictation will be by phrases marked above each melody ⌐‾‾‾‾‾⌐ . The only acceptable change in this phrasing is to lengthen the phrases if the class is capable of memorizing larger units.

It is very important that the student recognize the problem of writing the correct tempo. The impressions given by the same rhythmic pattern written once in $\frac{2}{4}$ and another time in $\frac{2}{2}$ are known to all of us. But the student will tend to make automatic, snap decisions about the unit of measurement. He will try to write everything in quarter metre. It is the teacher's problem to keep the student aware of the need to choose the proper metre, not only in the beat but also in the choice of unit of measurement. If the student is made aware of this need, he will be well on his way toward the development of his aesthetic sense of tempo. A practicing musician in any of the branches of music will find that a sense of tempo is a cornerstone of successful craftsmanship and artistry.

## *Rhythm*

Intone the following rhythmic patterns:

$\frac{3}{8}$ (1) ♪ ♪ ♪ | ♪ ♫♪ | ♪ ♪♪ | ♫ ♪ ♪ ‖

(2) ♪. | ♪ ♪. ♪ | ♩ ♫ | ♪ ♪. ♪ | ♩ ‖

(3) ♫ | ♫♪ ♫ | ♫♪. ♪ | ♫ ♫ | ♩ ‖

(4) ♫♫ | ♪. ♪♫ | ♫ ♫♪ | ♪♩ ⁷ ‖

(5) ♫♫♫ | ♫♪ ♪ | ♫♫♪ | ♩. ‖

(6) ♫ ♩ | ♩. ♫♩ | ⁷ ♪♫ | ♩.♫ | ♫⁷ | ♩. ‖

$\frac{3}{4}$ (7) ♪♩ ♪♩ | ♪♩ ♪ ♫ | ♫ ♩ ♫ | ♩ ♩ ‖

(8) ♪♩ ♪ ♫♫ | ♪♩ ♪ ♫ | ♫ ♩ ♫ | ♩. ‖

(9) ♩ ♫ ♫ | ♫ ♫ ♫ | ♩ ♪ ♫ | ♩. ‖

(10) ♪♩ ♫♩ | ♪♩ ♫♩ | ♪♩ ♫♫ | ♫ ♩ ‖

(11) ♫. ♩ ♫. ♩ | ♫ ♩ | ♫♩ ♫. ♩ | ♫♩ ‖

(12) ♪ | ♩ ♪♩ ♫ | ♫♩ ♫♫ | ♩ ♪♩ ♫ | ♩ ⁷ ‖

$\frac{5}{4}$ (13) ♩ ♩ ♩ ♩ | ♩ ♩ ♩ ♫ ♩ | ♩. ♪♩ ♫ ♫ ♩ | ♩. ‖

(14) ♫ ♩ ♫ ♩. ♪ | ♫ ♩ ♫ ♩ | ♪♩ ♪ ♫ ♩ ♩ | ♩ ♩. ‖

(15) ♩. ♫♫ ♫ ♩ | ♩. ♫ ♫ ♫ | ♩. ♩ ♫ | ♫. ‖

(16) ♩ ♩ ♩ ♩ ♩ | ♫ ♩ ♫ ♩ | ♫ ♩ | ♫ ♫ | ♩. ♪♩ ♩ ‖

### Measurement of Distance

Between any two tones there is a measurable distance. Two successively or simultaneously sounded tones are said to form an interval. At this time we must learn how to measure intervals so that they can be identified simply and quickly. In your musical studies after the first year, in the study of harmony, counterpoint, analysis, composition, and the like, you will be working constantly with simultaneously sounding tones. These will be in compositions of two or more parts. In our work, since we are concerned mainly with one voice we work with intervals sounded successively. Any distance, be it a leap, or a stepwise movement, is a measurable interval.

If the second tone is the same as the first the interval is a *prime*.

In measuring distances greater than a prime, count the letter names from one tone to the other, inclusive.

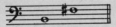

The letter names are B C D E F. Therefore, from B to F# is a 5th.

is a 10th (DEFGABCDEF), an octave plus a 2d.

Measure the following intervals.

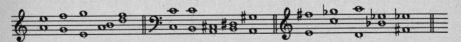

This is a rough measurement of intervals. The numbers that signify the interval's size will have to be qualified to become an exact measure.

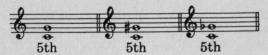

All these are 5ths. Clearly, the 5th from C to G# is larger than the 5th C — G. And C — Gb is smaller than C — G.

Intervals are divided into two groups. In the first group are 4ths, 5ths, and octaves.

In the second group are 2ds, 3rds, 6ths, and 7ths.

*Group I* — 4ths, 5ths, and octaves.

When the upper tone is in the major key of the lower tone (the lower tone is considered as the tonic), the interval is called *Perfect*.

An interval one-half step larger than Perfect is called *augmented*.

An interval one-half step smaller than Perfect is called *diminished*. Example:

*Group II* — 2ds, 3rds, 6ths, and 7ths.

When the upper tone is in the major key of the lower tone (the lower tone is considered as the tonic), the interval is called *Major*.

An interval one-half step larger than Major is called *augmented*.

An interval one-half step smaller than Major is called *minor*.

An interval one-half step smaller than Minor is called *diminished*. Example:

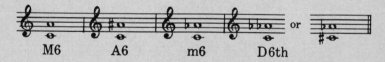

Every interval, then, must be measured for both size and quality. With both qualifications we have an exact measuring tool. Measure the intervals on the preceding page for both size and quality.

The following are the intervals that you will meet most often.

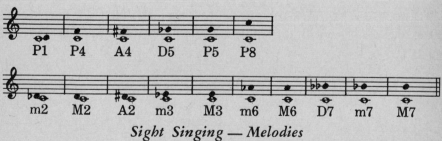

### Sight Singing — Melodies

In the following melodies mark all the passing tones, neighbors, and scale passages.

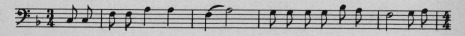

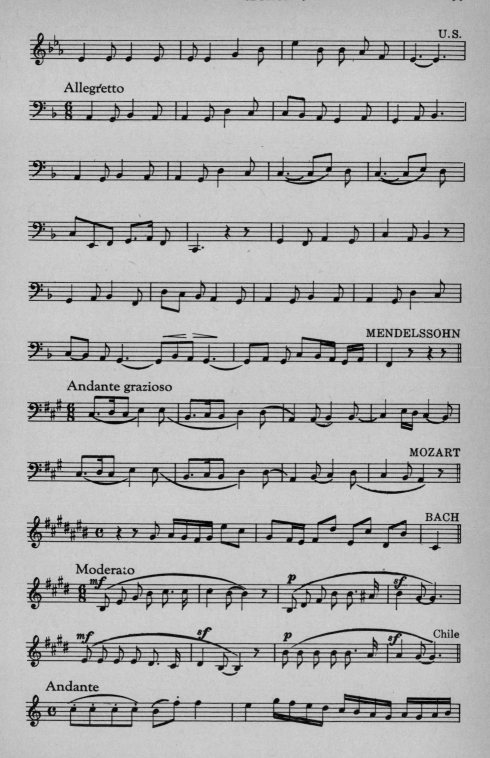

1 Reprinted by permission of Boosey & Hawkes, Inc., New York, New York.

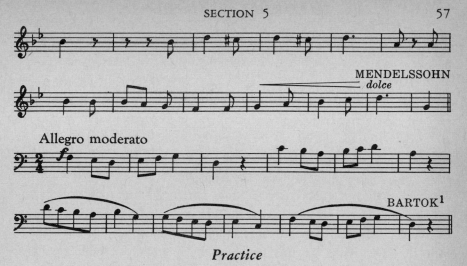

MENDELSSOHN
*dolce*

Allegro moderato

BARTOK[1]

## Practice

Your daily practice now includes the singing of major scales in three, four, five, six, seven, and eight metres in continuous patterns ascending and descending. Now begin the practice of these same exercises in the minor tonalities using the natural minor scales.

In practicing your own creative exercises in tone combinations try the following in all keys, major and minor.

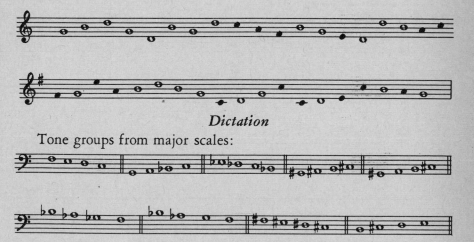

## Dictation

Tone groups from major scales:

The following melodies will be played for dictation. They will be played one phrase at a time. Memorize each section before you write the notes, and follow the dictation procedure outlined in Section 2 very carefully. You will be told the key of each melody; you will have to decide the metre, the tones, and the tempo.

1 Reprinted by permission of Boosey & Hawkes, Inc., New York, New York.

It will not be too difficult to decide whether you hear a two, three, six, or other beat. But it will be difficult to decide whether the metre should be $\frac{2}{4}$ or $\frac{2}{8}$ ; $\frac{3}{4}$ or $\frac{3}{8}$ ; $\frac{6}{4}$ or $\frac{6}{8}$ ; and so on. Don't just choose any unit of measurement at random; ♩ , ♪, or ♪ You must attempt to match on paper the sounds you hear in the music. Always think that what you write may be re-created by a performer who is looking to see what you mean. Every composer has had the task of putting on paper exactly or nearly exactly what he meant. Beethoven, in his sketches, indicates great doubt at times whether a movement of a symphony should be written in $\frac{3}{4}$ or $\frac{3}{8}$ . He tried each to see what feeling of correct tempo and mood came from the written page. It is important that you recognize this problem. Ultimately you will solve the problem by meeting it consciously each time you take dictation.

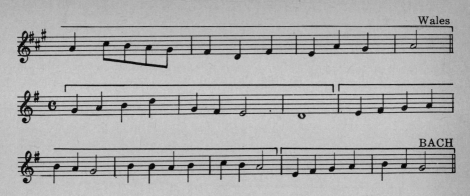

# Section 6.

Section 6 like Section 5 is a drill section. The emphasis during this section's work should be on students' practice methods. A new scale practice method is outlined. It involves singing all the major scales from one tone. If any one exercise could be singled out as most effective in aiding musical growth, this would be it. A thorough use of the exercise can lead to the point at which the teacher will sound the tonality at the beginning of a recitation hour, and the class will be able to follow all exercises, drills, and so on, for the rest of the hour, establishing the correct keys for dictation, sight singing melodies, and the like. We suggest that you explain this scale exercise thoroughly and drill the class completely before it takes the exercise as part of the daily practice routine.

Section 6 covers the following:

Practice
   Drill: all scales from one tone
Sight singing: melodies
   Rhythmic patterns to be intoned
Dictation
   Scale patterns from major scales
   Melodies

## *Practice*

You should now have a working familiarity with the major scale. The major scale exercises used thus far may now be dropped; continue them in minor tonalities. The following exercises should be begun in major; later on these too will be done in minor. These exercises will be more difficult than preceding ones and will yield many lasting results.

*Drill*: *all scales from one tone*

From the tone C to the octave above and below sing the following major scales: C, Db, Eb, F, G, Ab, Bb.

These are the major scales that use the common tone "C." You will have to think carefully in singing these to establish the whole steps and the half steps correctly. The remaining major scales will be sung in the octave from C#. These will be D, E, F#, A, and B majors.

In preparing the first group of seven scales sound only C on an instrument. In preparing the second group of five scales sound only C# on an instrument.

Practice the scales above from C and C# for one week. Then practice the scales from D — D# — Db, E — E# — Eb, F — F#, G — G#, A — A# — Ab, B — Bb. After four weeks, which will take you through the scales in the F octave, sing all the scales each day within a different octave.

Continue with the daily exercises for the increase of tone combinations.

### Sight Singing — Melodies

1 Reprinted by permission of Boosey & Hawkes, Inc., New York, New York.

Lento

espressivo

BACH

sost.

BRAHMS

dim.

U.S.

Chile

## Rhythm

Intone the following rhythmic patterns:

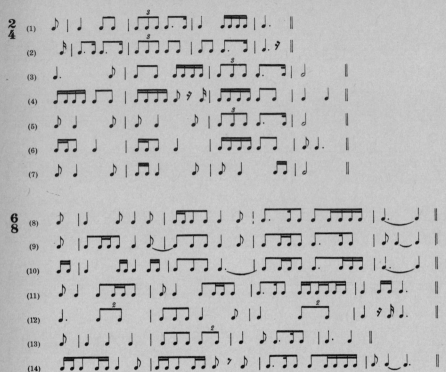

## Dictation

Scale patterns from major scales:

Melodies:

BACH

France

Germany

England

BACH

# Section 7.

Section 7 covers the following:

Rhythmic patterns to be intoned
Practice
    Major scales from one tone
Phrasing
Sight singing: melodies
Dictation
    Tone groups from major scales

Melodies
In explaining phrasing and the marking of phrases, the teacher should attempt to reinforce and refine the natural ability of most students to phrase melodies. Constant attention must be drawn to the importance of using musical punctuation in order to perform clearly. We feel that it is very important that the teacher analyze the elements and structure of phrases as carefully as we have done in this section. This procedure strengthens and encourages the students' innate musicality with reason and musical logic.

*Practice.* We continue with the major scales from one tone. This may still require class drill before the student can practice on his own.

## Rhythm
Intone the following rhythmic patterns:

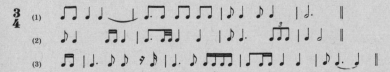

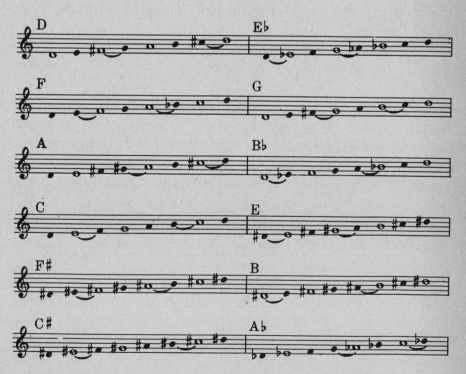

## Practice

Continue your daily practice of major scales from one tone. From
D — D# — Db the scales will be as follows:

Try the following exercise in practicing tone combinations in all keys, major and minor.

## Phrasing

We return once more to our definition of music as the movement of sound in time to seek a fuller understanding of this movement. We have been using some of the elements of sound and rhythm in training our musical reflexes. It is time now to see how these elements are combined in the motion of a complete melody.

The motion of a complete composition is ultimately mirrored in the individual movements from one tone to the next. In between the total and the smallest parts are patterns of organization that lead to the image of the whole. One of the most important of these patterns is called a *phrase*.

A phrase is comparable to a sentence, except that it need not complete a meaning and may not be followed by a complete stop. A phrase is much more a complete sentence followed by a semicolon. The phrase consists of one or more characteristic *motives* arranged so that the energy for musical movement begins at the beginning of the phrase and ends or *cadences* at the end of the phrase, only to be extended, renewed, and developed in following phrases.

The following melody is in two phrases, outlined by the marks ⌒ ⌒ .

There is a natural lapse after G of measure four followed by a renewal of activity until the conclusion and final cadence of the melody. The first phrase sets the characteristic rhythmic and tonal *motives*. The rhythmic *motives* include the up-beat

and the dotted rhythm

The first phrases consist of two *motives* each outlined by the marking ⌊＿＿＿＿⌋ under the melody.

An outline of the melodic action of the first phrase looks as follows:

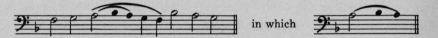

is a neighboring note figure, and

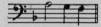

is a cadence that is not final. The first phrase cadences on G, the 2nd degree in the key of F major. It is so active a tone that the melody must continue to its ultimate conclusion in the next phrase.

The melodic outline of the second phrase is:

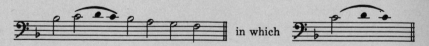

is a neighboring note figure. So, the complete melody in two phrases

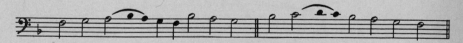

shows us the function of each part. The first begins a movement from F up to B♭ and falls incompletely. The second picks up at B♭, moves one step higher to C, and then cadences completely to the tonic. In this melody the climax is reached on the C neighboring note figure, and with the arrival of the climax the conflict is resolved to the stable key tone.

The following melody has four phrases:

In your sight singing from this point on mark all the phrases. Perform the melodies so that the beginning of the phrases has a subtle "push" of energy and the close tapers off. But sing the melody as a continuous structure.

*It is not necessary that you outline the rhythmic and tonal movement as we have done above.*

You will be able to recognize the phrases after singing each melody. The analysis of melodic structure will be a major portion of our later work.

### *Sight Singing — Melodies*

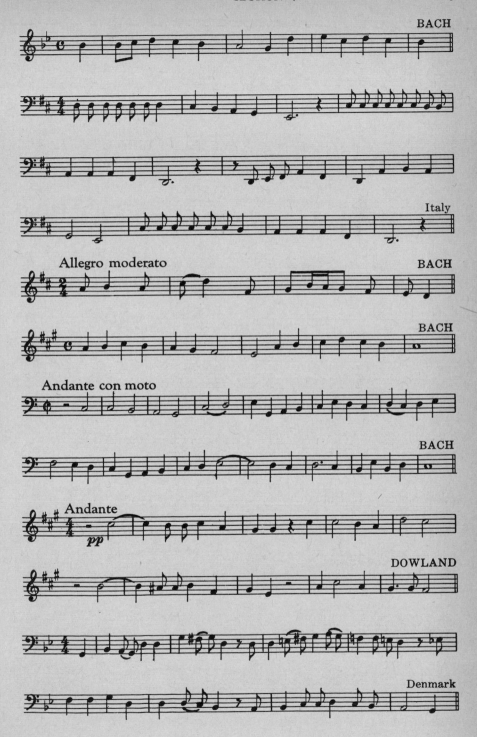

1 Reprinted by permission of Boosey & Hawkes, Inc., New York, New York.

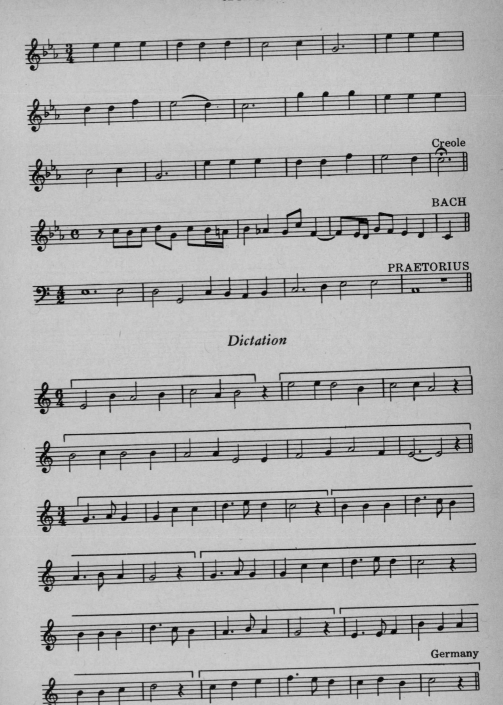

Creole

BACH

PRAETORIUS

*Dictation*

Germany

Section 8 covers

Practice
  Major scales fron
  Exercise in tone
Rhythm
  Patterns to be in
  Unmeasured melc
Sight singing: melc
Dictation
  Melodies

*Practice.* Major s
stood by this time.
pulate these scales w
  *Rhythm.* We intro
This is essentially a
two melodies in class
  *Sight singing.* It i
the phrases, scale pas
and more insistent t
the melodic meaning
structural analysis to
of phrasing, tempo, d

Continue practicing
E# the major scales an

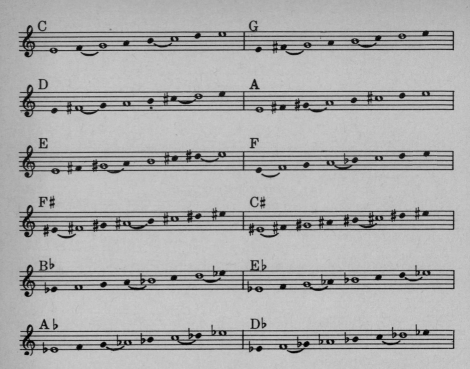

Try the following exercise in tone combinations; major and minor keys.

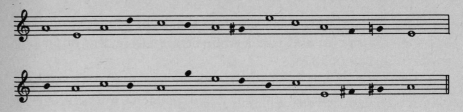

## Rhythm

Intone the following rhythmic patterns:

Indicate the metre and the position of the bar lines of each of the following melodies.

*Sight Singing — Melodies*

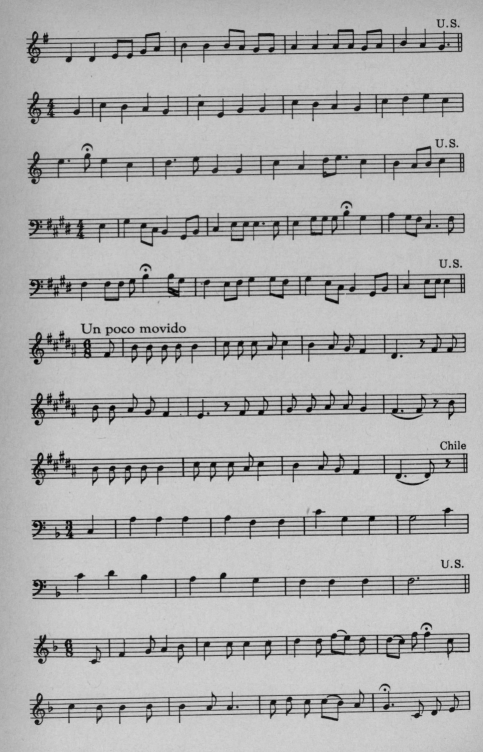

## Dictation — Melodies

France

BACH

Scotland

Tyrol

# Section 9.

Sections 9 and 10 are again drill sections; all the work should be prepared and performed in class. These two sections will consummate the first part of the year's work. The following material is covered in these sections:

Rhythm
  Patterns from compositions; to be intoned
  Unmeasured melodies, indication of the metre and bar lines by students
Sight singing: melodies
Dictation: melodies

*Rhythm.* Instead of the type of concentrated rhythmic patterns we have used thus far, we now substitute patterns taken from compositions. These will present a wide variety of rhythmic patterns in groups longer than the four measures we have been using. The attempt should be to establish a rhythmic flow. This will be aided if the student will beat only the first beat of each measure.

## Rhythm

Intone the following:

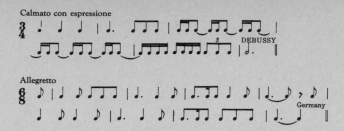

Indicate the metre and the position of bar lines of each of the following melodies:

### Sight Singing — Melodies

**Andante con moto**

MENDELSSOHN

BACH

U.S.

## Dictation — Melodies

Switzerland

Scotland

England

Tyrol

# Section 10.

*Rhythm*

Intone the following:

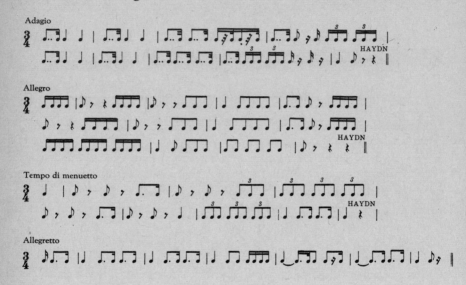

Indicate the metre and the position of the bar lines of each of the
following melodies:

*Sight Singing — Melodies*

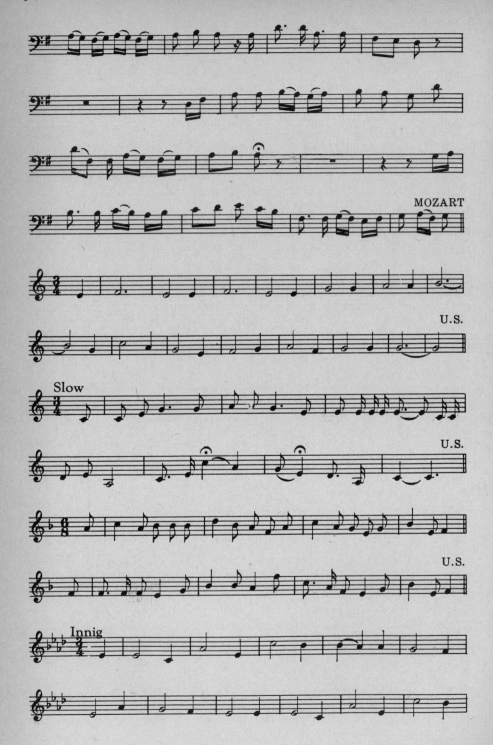

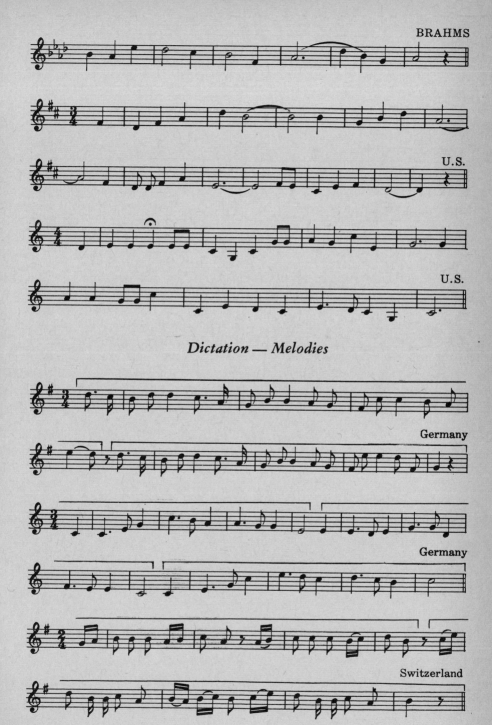

BRAHMS

U.S.

U.S.

*Dictation — Melodies*

Germany

Germany

Switzerland

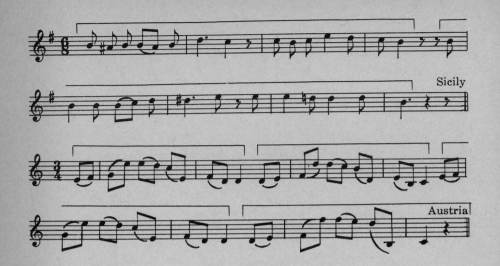

Sicily

Austria

# Part II

## *Introduction*

You have now completed the first half of this elementary study in musicianship. Some of the lessons of the first ten sections are completely learned. Others are still in the process of assimilation. It will be that way in all your musical experiences. You will be gaining new skills while others are settling in your mind.

By this time the identification of notes on the treble and bass staves is no longer a problem. Basic concepts of metre and the performance of many rhythmic figures are already set. You know the major and the minor scales, but they are far from complete tools as yet. Your ability in sight singing and taking dictation of simple melodies has begun to grow. These will all be used continually throughout our studies.

One estimate of accomplishment, however, must come from you alone. Have you developed a disciplined system of orderly practice? Are you aware at each point in your practicing of what you are trying to accomplish? Does your practicing include much wasted, unconcentrated time? Have you learned to solve new problems with the knowledge and techniques you already have?

Other than the acquisition of some of the simplest basic skills, the most important task of beginning musicians is to develop a disciplined musical approach. Always keep in mind the importance of performing each work fully, be it a short melody or a full symphony. If you learn to perceive and perform the complete meanings of melodies during this year, the expression of larger and grander musical ideas will be very much easier.

# Section 11.

===============================================

### Notes To The Teacher

With the beginning of the second part of the course in elementary musicianship, it is of paramount importance that the teacher take stock of what is already accomplished. This should have been done in the work of Sections 9 and 10. If some time elapses between the first and second terms, it might be wise to review the last two sections before going ahead.

Of the new material to be taught in Part II, there are two major elements: the study of intervals and the analysis of melodic movement. Other new work develops more directly from the preceding sections and concerns chromaticism, modulation, transposition, and the C clefs.

The compositions in the appendix will be particularly useful from this point on. The regular sight singing study should be supplemented by impromptu choral sessions using rounds, canons, and part compositions. The performance of these by the class will satisfy the need in students for a sense of accomplishment. The aesthetic satisfaction in singing complete compositions involves an important broadening of student musical perspectives. Fit the choral sessions into the scheme of lessons as you deem wise. Some teachers may want to establish regular periods of group singing. Others may want to use choral techniques to give the class a lift at strategic points in the term's work. No matter how the compositions are utilized, the emphasis on larger and more complete aesthetic experiences must be made.

Section 11 covers the following:

Intervals
  Drills
  Dictation

Practice
    Review of major scales from one tone
    Minor scales from one tone
    Intervals
Rhythm
    Unmeasured melodies; indication of metre and bar lines by students
    Patterns from compositions to be intoned
Sight singing: melodies
Dictation: melodies

*Intervals.* We approach the problem of intervals in two ways. First come the hearing and manipulation of intervals conceived absolutely, i.e., as a space measured in terms of the major key of the lower tone. The next few weeks' work will continue on this basis solely. Then we begin to work with the intervals as they appear in major and minor tonalities. It is vital in teaching intervals that students be taught a method in singing and measuring leaps. The major scale pattern is the best tool for measurement, and by this time the student can already think in major with some facility. If you adhere to the method strictly, the usual student feeling of being overwhelmed by interval study will be avoided.

## Intervals

An interval exists whenever two tones are sounded, either simultaneously or successively. The interval between two tones is the distance that separates them. In Section 5, the measurement of intervals was explained. If you are able to measure intervals on the printed page, your studies in the sound and manipulation of intervals will be facilitated. Review the explanations in Section 5.

## Drill

Write all the intervals on page 106 from each of the twelve tones.

We study the sound, structure, and nature of intervals for two reasons. First, intervals are always present in music, even in the simplest one-voice compositions. We must know all the intervals to be able to read as well as to develop an understanding through listening. Second, the study of intervals is the initial preparation for future studies of music more complex than one-voice melodies. An interval

sounded simultaneously is already two voices. The disciplines of harmony and counterpoint lead to an understanding of three-, four-, five-
voice and even more complex music. Our work with intervals will approach the study of more complex musical structures.

Intervals are measured for size and quality in terms of the major
key of the lower tone. Whenever an interval is to be measured, even
in a composition, one can measure accurately through the major key
of the lower tone, which is therefore considered (for the moment) the
tonic. In a composition in E♭ major, for example, the interval from
F ♮ up to D ♮ will be measured from F in the key of F major. The
interval is a Major sixth, since D is in the key of F major, and six
letter names separate the tones (F, G, A, B, C, D).

*Drill*

Measure the following intervals:

In the following melody measure the intervals between each tone
and the following tone:

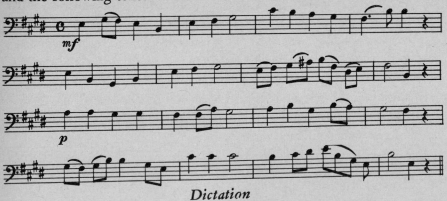

*Dictation*

The following intervals will be dictated. Think the lower tone, think
the upper tone, then measure the distance between by singing up the
major scale of the lower tone. Since not all intervals are Major or
Perfect in quality, you will have to manipulate the changes in half
steps from the major scale.

In this dictation write only the size and quality of the intervals sounded.

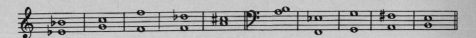

In the following interval dictation the teacher will identify the lower or the upper tones. You are to write the other tones and the size and quality of the interval.

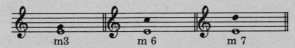

The minor 3rd, 6th, and 7th all appear in the pure minor scale.

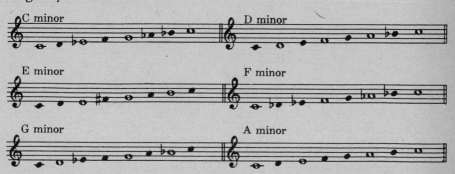

m3          m 6          m 7

As you become more familiar with the intervals, you will be able to measure these minor intervals directly from the minor scale.

### Practice

(1) Review and sing all *major* scales from one tone.

(2) Sing all minor scales from one tone. During the first week sing only in the octave C — C.

C minor          D minor

E minor          F minor

G minor          A minor

(3) Measure and sing the following intervals. Sound the lower tone on a piano, and sing up the scale until you sing the upper tone. Then sing the leap from the lower tone to the upper tone. *Also sing DOWN from the upper tone to the lower.*

Example:                          Sing:

 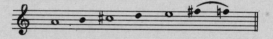

In A major, sing up to F# and then down to F ♮ , a half step. Since F# is the 6th degree of the A major scale, the interval A — F ♮ is a minor 6th (m6).

### *Rhythm*

Indicate the metre and the position of the bar lines in each of the following melodies.

Intone the following rhythmic patterns:

## *Sight Singing — Melodies*

France

Andante
*mf*

U.S.

Armenia

Austria

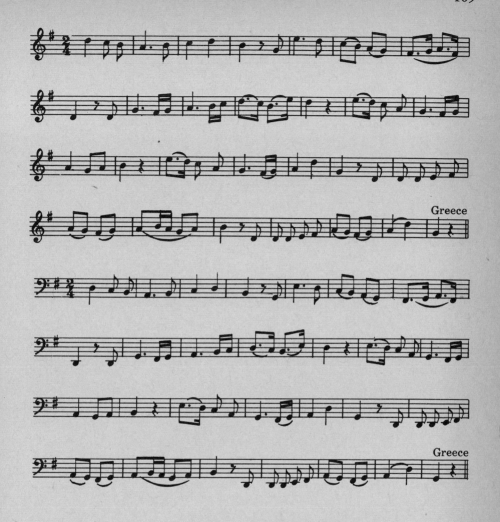

Greece

Greece

## Dictation — Melodies

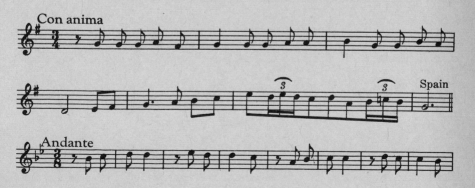

Con anima

Spain

Andante

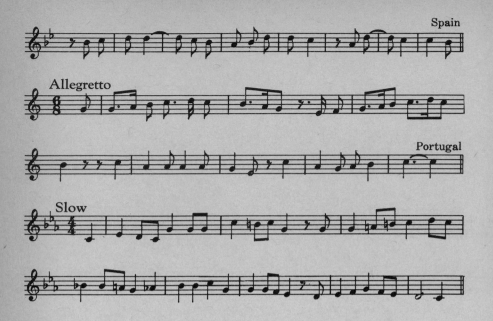

# Section 12.

---

Section 12 is a drill section. The concentration of work in class will enable you to guarantee that practice procedures are integrated and that the approach to intervals is understood.

It is most important to remind the student and dwell on the problem of writing the tempo indications of dictation melodies accurately. This problem was stated in Section 5 when melodic dictation was begun. The students should already evidence a growing aesthetic of tempo. The renewed emphasis on this problem anticipates the dictation of more difficult and more subtle melodies.

Section 12 covers the following:

Practice
  Minor scales from one tone
  Major scales from one tone; two octaves
  Intervals
Rhythm
  Patterns from compositions to be intoned
  Unmeasured melodies; indication of metre and bar lines by students
Intervals: measurement drill
Dictation
  Intervals
  Melodies
Sight singing: melodies

### Practice

Sing the minor scales from one tone. From D — D# — D♭ they will be as follows:

Sing the major scales from one tone. Extend the scales over two octaves. In singing the second octave you will find that the key tone asserts itself strongly.

Measure and sing the following intervals:

## *Rhythm*

Intone the following patterns:

Indicate the metre and bar lines in each of the following melodies:

## Intervals — Measurement Drill

Complete the following intervals above and below the given notes:

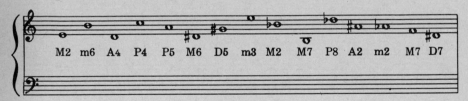

M2  m6  A4  P4  P5  M6  D5  m3  M2  M7  P8  A2  m2  M7  D7

## Dictation

**Intervals**

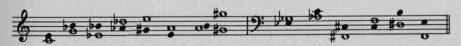

**Melodies**

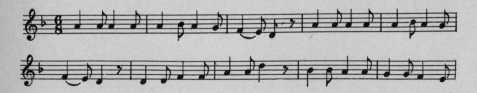

## Sight Singing — Melodies

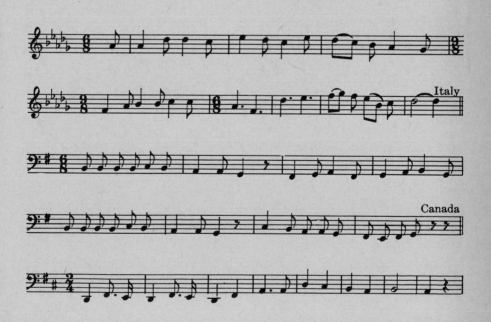

Canada

Canada

Ireland

England

U.S.

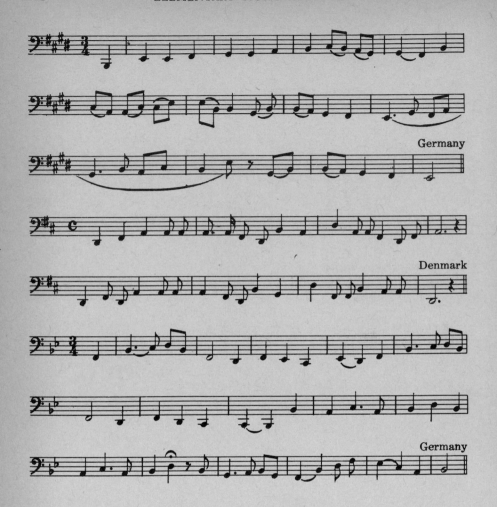

Germany

Denmark

Germany

# Section 13.

*Intervals.* We begin the study of intervals within the scales. Though the exact placement of intervals within the major and minor tonalities may be new to the students, the sounds of the intervals from the various scale degrees will have been experienced. This experience, gained through the sight singing and melodic dictation work, must be refined and made exact.

There is one drill in Section 13 that requires the teacher's aid. The teacher will play indicated chords; students will sing intervals above and below the top and bass tones of the chords. This drill will strengthen the grasp of absolute intervals. The chords are constructed to avoid the feeling of tonality in completing the intervals.

*Practice.* The new exercise for home practice involves singing major scales *down* from a common tone. The common tone is to be considered one of the scale degrees; the scale is to be sung *down* to the tonic.

### Rhythm

Intone the following patterns:

Indicate the metre and bar lines in each of the following melodies:

SCHUBERT

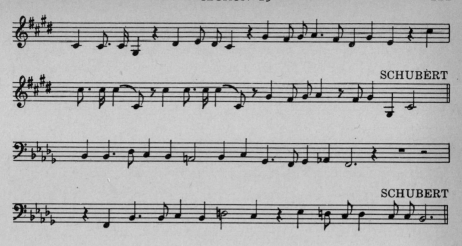

SCHUBERT

SCHUBERT

## *Sight Singing — Melodies*

F. ZELTER

Zart bewegt

BRAHMS

Belgium

**Allegro**

MOZART

MOZART

PRAETORIUS

**Andante**

MENDELSSOHN

**Bewegt und leise**

BRAHMS

## Intervals

### Intervals relative to tonalities

Parallel with our consideration of intervals measured absolutely we shall examine and hear the position of intervals within the major and minor tonalities. All the intervals occur within the major and minor scales. The Perfect 5th can be heard from the 1st to the 5th degrees of the major scale; or from the 2nd to the 6th degrees. The minor 2nd can be heard from the 3rd to the 4th degrees of the major scale, and so on. We shall continue working with intervals absolutely while we study these interval relationships within the scales. Our ability to hear and differentiate the feeling of each scale degree will be a great help in establishing interval recognition within major and minor tonalities. The effect of the knowledge of intervals within the tonalities is far reaching. You will find this knowledge useful not only in basic skills like reading, but also in much more advanced disciplines, including whatever work you may do in composition.

## The perfect 5th in major and minor scales

The Perfect 5th appears in the major scale between the following scale degrees:

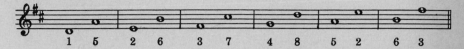

1  5      2  6      3  7      4  8      5  2      6  3

The Perfect 5th appears in the minor scale between the following scale degrees:

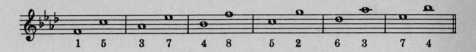

1  5      3  7      4  8      5  2      6  3      7  4

## Drill

In E major sing a Perfect 5th above the given tones; write the correct tone; name the scale degree.

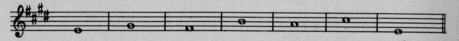

In Bb major sing a Perfect 5th below the given tones; write the correct tone; name the scale degree.

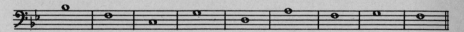

In C minor sing a Perfect 5th above the given tones; write the correct tone; name the scale degree.

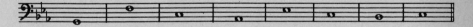

In F# minor sing a Perfect 5th below the given tones; write the correct tone; name the scale degree.

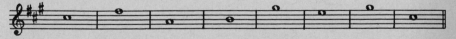

## Absolute intervals

Measure and sing the following intervals above and below the given tones:

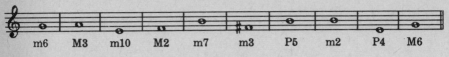

m6    M3    m10    M2    m7    m3    P5    m2    P4    M6

## Drill

The teacher will sound the following chords on the piano. Students will sing a Major 3rd above each of the top notes of the chords, and a Perfect 5th below each of the lowest tones of the chords.

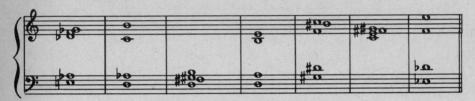

## Dictation

### Intervals

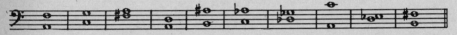

### Melodies

MOZART

MENDELSSOHN

SCHUMANN

SCHUBERT

## Practice

Continue singing minor scales from one tone. The minor scales from
E — E♭ — E# are as follows:

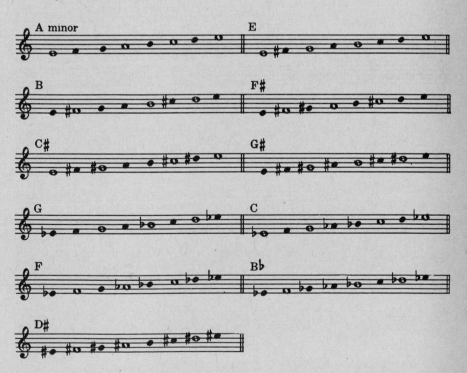

## *Major scales down from one tone*

Sound the tone B; consider B the 5th degree of the major scale (E major); sing down to the tonic.

Now consider B the 7th tone (C major); sing down to the tonic.

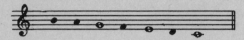

From B and Bb the scales down from one tone will be as follows:

# Section 14.

*Notes To The Teacher*

Section 14 covers the following:

Rhythm
  Patterns from compositions to be intoned
Modulation
  Concept
  Application to sight singing
Sight singing: melodies
Dictation
  Four-note major and minor scale groups
  Absolute intervals
  Melodies
Intervals
  Major and minor 3rds
Practice
  Minor scales from one tone
  Major scales down from one tone
  Intervals within major and minor keys

*Modulation.* Though it is not possible to explain modulation completely without a knowledge of harmonic progressions, the awareness of modulation in melodies can be sharpened. Harmonic progressions often support and realize modulations already implied in melodic movement. It is especially important for beginning music students to hear these implications of key change. In the writing of harmonic exercises, indeed, even in much later work, the students' ability to hear melodic modulations will lead them to richness of resources and skill in manipulation that always result from hearing before writing.

*Dictation.* We repeat the dictation of four-note scale groups. Now the student will be asked to identify two tonalities for each scale group. This dictation exercise should be done twice; once for major and once for minor tonalities.

## Rhythm

Intone the following patterns:

$4 + \frac{2}{8} + 3$    [rhythmic notation]   BARTOK[1]

[rhythmic notation]

$2 + \frac{2}{8} + 3$    [rhythmic notation]   BARTOK[1]

[rhythmic notation]

$3 + \frac{2}{8} + 3$    [rhythmic notation]   BARTOK[1]

[rhythmic notation]

$2 + 2 + \frac{2}{8} + 3$    [rhythmic notation]   BARTOK[1]

[rhythmic notation]

## Modulation

### Concept

Modulation is the technique of changing tonal centers within a composition. The process of moving from one key to another is the modulation.

The technique of modulation is used in compositions as an expressive device to establish contrast and development. You have already witnessed other contrasts, in rhythmic and melodic *motives*. These contrasts or conflicts are the sources of musical movement in that they create tension, interest, climax, and, ultimately, resolution. The contrasts of different keys widen the palette of compositional color. Modulations are used in their most extended and complete applications in large compositions, rarely if at all in folk songs. The first movements of classical symphonies and sonatas are essentially built on the contrast of key centers.

A sudden change of key produces a highly dramatic effect. This use will often be found in operas, songs, and so forth.

---

1 Reprinted by permission of Boosey & Hawkes, Inc., New York, New York.

### Application to sight singing

In your sight singing you will feel when a new key center becomes established.

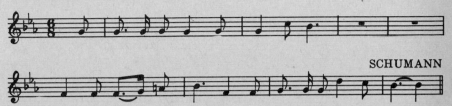

SCHUMANN

In the second phrase of the Schumann song we feel that the tonal center shifts from E♭ to B♭. In the process of moving between keys the accidentals of the new key are introduced. In that area where the modulation is taking place there may often be a lack of clear key feeling. You can understand the great importance of hearing and manipulating intervals exactly in these transitional areas. The dependence on key feeling is cut loose and an ability with intervals will keep the music moving until new moorings are established.

The most musically intelligent way to keep one's bearings throughout a composition is to understand its movement—to be able to answer the questions: "From where does the motion come?" "Where does the motion go?" For the moment we shall delay the treatment of this master of musical problems until you are comfortable with more of the basic theoretical and structural techniques.

### Sight Singing — Melodies

ZELTER

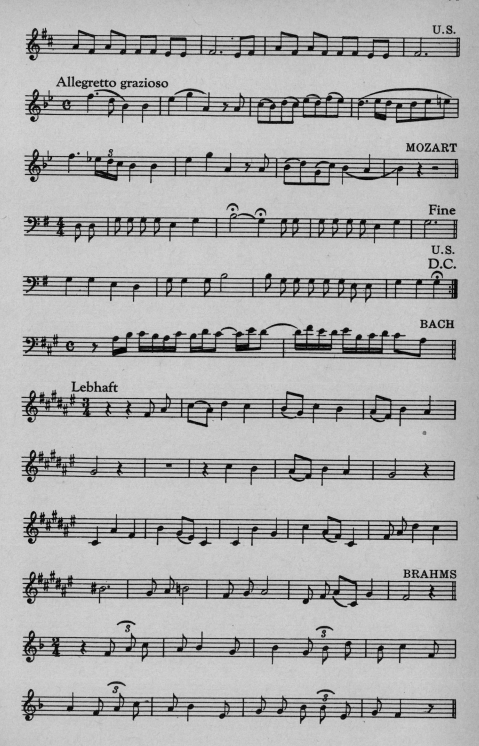

1 Reprinted by permission of Boosey & Hawkes, Inc., New York, New York.

## Dictation

### Four-note major and minor scale groups

The following groups of four notes from major and minor scales
will be played. Students are to write the numbers of the scale degrees
that are represented. Each example can be set in two different keys, so
that there will be two answers for each dictation group.

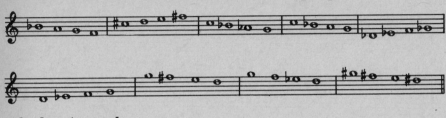

### Absolute intervals

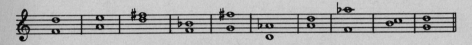

The following intervals will be dictated in the key of E♭ major.
Establish the key center before beginning.

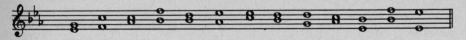

### Melodies

SCHUBERT

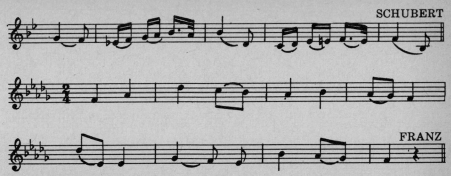

SCHUBERT

FRANZ

## Major and minor 3rds

The Major 3rd appears in the major scale between the following scale degrees:

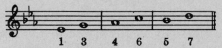

The Major 3rd appears in the minor scale between the following scale degrees:

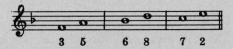

The minor 3rd appears in the major scale between the following scale degrees:

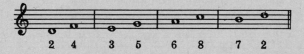

The minor 3rd appears in the minor scale between the following scale degrees:

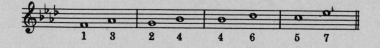

Measure and sing the following intervals as indicated:

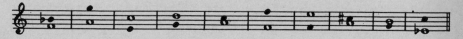

## Drill

The teacher will sound the following chords on the piano. Students will sing a minor 3rd above each of the top tones of the chords, and a Major 3rd below each of the lowest tones of the chords.

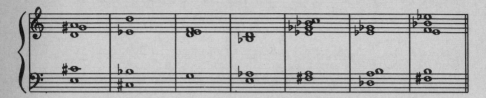

## Practice

Continue singing the minor scales from one tone. By now you should be using a different base tone each day so that within one week all the tones are used as base tones.

## Major scales down from one tone

From D — Db — D# the scales will be as follows:

## Intervals within major and minor keys

In the following keys sing Major and minor 3rds above and below the given tones; write the correct tones; name the scale degrees.

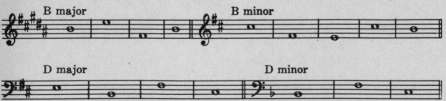

# Section 15.

Section 15 covers the following:

Rhythm
  Patterns from compositions to be intoned
Chromaticism
Sight singing: melodies
Dictation
  Four-note scale groups in major and minor
  Absolute intervals
  Intervals in G major
  Melodies
Intervals
  The Perfect 4th
Practice
  Minor scales from one tone
  Major and minor scales down from one tone-
  Intervals

*Chromaticism.* The student has been singing and hearing tones not included in the diatonic scale. The discussion of chromaticism should clarify this experience and lead the student to see the vast expanse of composition to which chromatic concepts have given rise. For this purpose many examples should be played in class — Wagner, Debussy, Schoenberg, Hindemith, and so on.

*Practice.* Training in intervals must be left more and more up to the student. Proficiency with intervals requires his intense and controlled attention. He should be given encouragement in arranging and emphasizing his practice to train himself at the weakest points.

## Rhythm

Intone the following patterns:

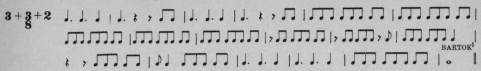

## Chromaticism

Chromaticism in compositions refers to the use of tones not included in the diatonic scale. The use of the tones G# and D# in a composition in D major would be considered chromaticisms, except if those tones foreign to D major were part of a modulation.

Chromatic tones are used for added color, emphasis, to fill in melodic movement, and so forth. Chromatics, that is, extra half steps, can be used so much that the feeling of tonal center is noticeably weakened, and sometimes completely obliterated. This happens in much of the music of Richard Wagner. We say of this music that it employs the chromatic or twelve-tone scale. The result of using the chromatic scale is comparable to the use of the natural minor scale, in which the whole step from the seventh to the tonic makes the feeling of tonal center much less predictable than in major. The arbitrary establishment of a key center in compositions using the chromatic scale is even more emphasized. In modern times the composer Arnold Schoenberg has formulated a system of composition based on the equal value of all the twelve tones. Hence, there would be no key center as the dominating tonality of his compositions. When mention is made of the twelve-tone system, it refers to the principles of Schoenberg and his followers.

In the following examples you will hear the use of chromaticism in filling in a melodic line (Chopin) and as part of the twelve-one system (Schoenberg).

**Semplice**

1 Reprinted by permission of Boosey & Hawkes, Inc., New York, New York.

*Sight Singing — Melodies*

CHOPIN

BRAHMS

HAYDN

BEETHOVEN

BRAHMS

## Dictation

### Four-note scale groups in major and minor

The following groups of four notes from major and minor scales will be played. Students are to write the numbers of the scale degrees that are represented. Each example can be set in two different keys in major and two in minor tonalities.

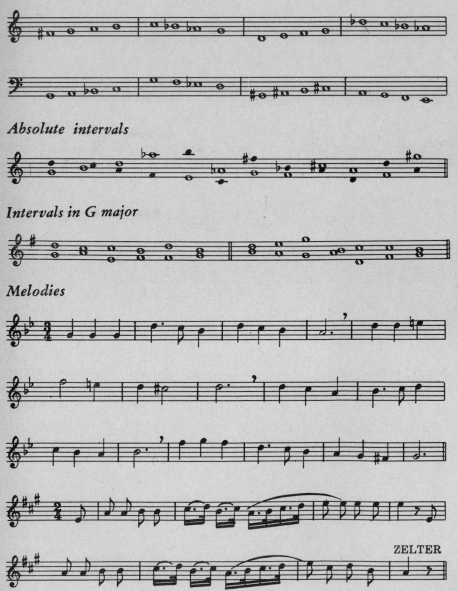

*Absolute intervals*

*Intervals in G major*

*Melodies*

ZELTER

ZELTER

Tempo di menuetto

BARTOK[1]

## Intervals

### The perfect 4th

The Perfect 4th appears in the major scale between the following scale degrees:

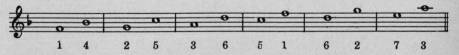

| 1 | 4 | | 2 | 5 | | 3 | 6 | | 5 | 1 | | 6 | 2 | | 7 | 3 |

The Perfect 4th appears in the minor scale between the following scale degrees:

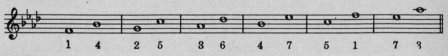

| 1 | 4 | | 2 | 5 | | 3 | 6 | | 4 | 7 | | 5 | 1 | | 7 | 3 |

### Drill

The teacher will sound the following chords on the piano. Students will sing a Perfect 4th above each of the top tones of the chords.

1 Reprinted by permission of Boosey & Hawkes, Inc., New York, New York.

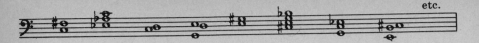

Sing a Perfect 4th below each of the lowest tones of the following chords:

### Practice

Continue singing the minor scales from one tone.

Continue singing major scales down from one tone; add the minor scales.

### Intervals

From this point on the practice of intervals and the creation of practice exercises will rest more completely in your hands. You know best what areas of work need the most concentration; which intervals are still incompletely heard; which intervals are difficult to sing. Each week's practice in intervals should include exercises like the following, which you will have to create for yourself in the remainder of the year's study.

Sing a Perfect 4th above and below each of the following notes:

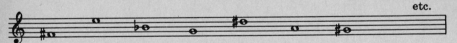

Sing a Major 3rd above and below each of the following notes:

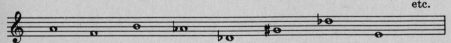

Sing a minor 3rd above and below each of the following notes:

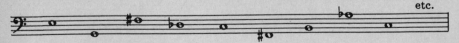

# Section 16

*Analysis.* The ultimate goal of all music training should be a conscious understanding of musical art works. In the next few sections we shall try to approach some of the larger problems of musical compositions utilizing the experiences and the craftsmanship of the student at this elementary stage of his training. If an art form is valid, it is so not only at the most complex levels of its activity but also at the simplest levels. To wait a few years until the student has gained more control of musical elements and theory would mean a denial of his artistic curiosity and his natural aesthetic growth. Our analysis will be strictly limited to what the student can handle; this is a challenging problem. Harmonic implications, contrapuntal voice leading, and similar aspects —these cannot be used. We are limited essentially to melodies. What must be explained in more advanced terms will be omitted.

The success of the analytical work depends very much on the teacher's presentation. Students have found this the most exciting portion of the course in musicianship. They gain not only a sense of dignity in the art but also a keener insight into the relationship between craft and composition.

### Sight Singing — Melodies

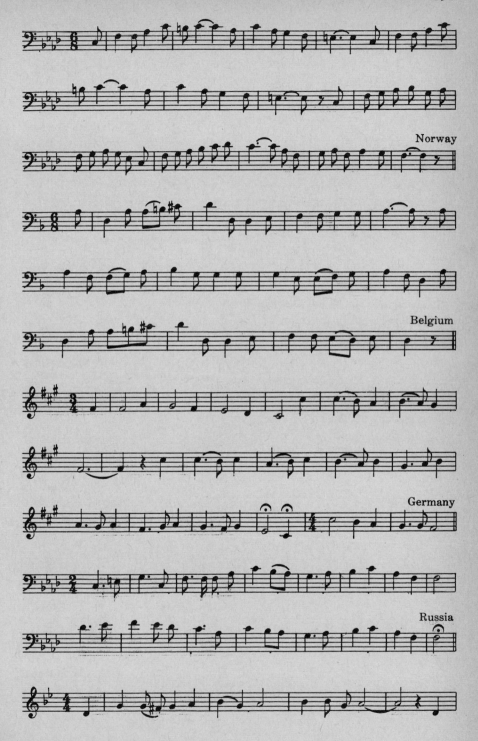

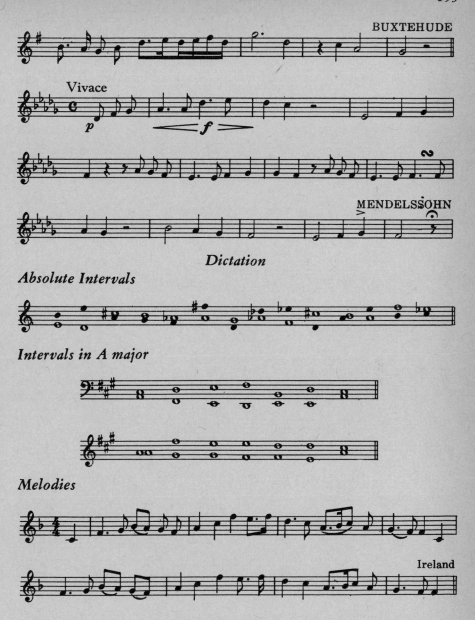

BUXTEHUDE

Vivace

MENDELSSOHN

## Dictation

*Absolute Intervals*

*Intervals in A major*

*Melodies*

Ireland

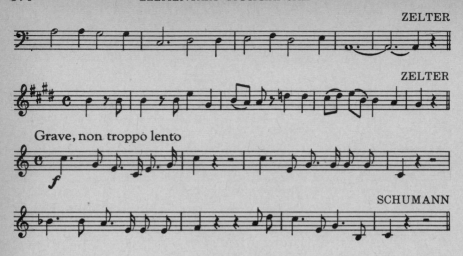

## Intervals

### The major 6th; the minor 6th

The Major 6th appears in the major and minor scales between the following scale degrees:

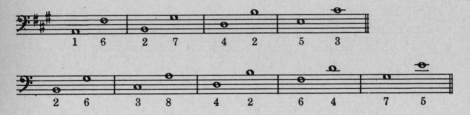

The minor 6th appears in the major and minor scales between the following scale degrees:

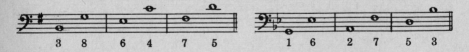

### Drill

Sing a Major 6th above and a minor 6th below the top and bottom tones, respectively, of the following chords:

etc.

Sing a minor 6th above and a Major 6th below the top and bottom tones, respectively, of the following chords:

## Inversion of intervals

All intervals can be inverted; i.e., using the same tones the position of the upper and lower tones can be exchanged.

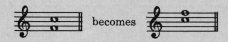

This is done by transferring one of the tones an octave. A Perfect 5th becomes a Perfect 4th.

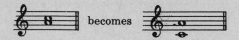

A 4th becomes a 5th; a 3rd becomes a 6th. Both intervals always add up to the number 9. A 2d becomes a 7th, and so on.

The qualities of the intervals also change. A Major 3rd becomes a minor 6th.

### INVERSION

| Major | becomes | minor |
|---|---|---|
| minor | becomes | Major |
| augmented | becomes | diminished |
| diminished | becomes | augmented |

*Perfect remains the same.* Through inversion, the Perfect 4th becomes a Perfect 5th.

## Drill

Invert the following intervals and identify the resultant intervals:

## Analysis

All art forms are sensible. At the height of effectiveness, they evidence a complete unity of conception and detail, and bear the closest scrutiny in objective terms. Too often we have difficulty in analyzing the meanings of art works because we are at a loss for descriptive and analytical terms to fit the medium. In forms that express themselves in time, music, drama, and so forth, descriptive terminology is especially difficult. Music and dance have suffered most in this respect. The drama much less so, because the expression of concepts involves the use of a common language with accepted and definable meanings.

The objective statement of musical meanings is important. It leads to and develops a musical intelligibility. We don't mean to deny or to belittle the intuitive and inspirational; without inspiration art would be dead. But the analysis and clarification of meanings support and refine the intuitive so that the creation and performance of compositions express most incisively latent emotional qualities.

In the craft of music we can always be objective. The reading of notes, the measurement of intervals, the fingering of instruments — these are measurable and clear. As far as one can go, the musician must attempt to understand as well as feel the meanings in musical compositions.

## Movement

Music involves the movement of tones in time. All compositions take a certain length of time to fulfill themselves. Compositions are incomplete until the last tone is sounded. The time element is divided and arranged in patterns that move along with and support or oppose the tonal elements — melodies, chords, and so on. The tonal elements in their turn must flow while filling up a length of time.

Motion in music is never of one kind. Sometimes a composition sounds as if it is moving very quickly; it may suddenly seem to move rather slowly — and all within the same beat. Two of the simplest types of motion are faster and slower. Often a composition may sound as if it is complicating the given material, or turning back on itself (leading to a restatement), or moving very little but ornamenting an idea, or it may evince movement in various other ways.

Below are a few examples that will be played for you. Within each example, no matter how short, there are contrasts of movement. You will listen and attempt to hear where the music seems to drive, where it relaxes, where it falls after a climax, where it "thickens," and so forth. After each example *state to the teacher* in what measures, and even in what particular notes, you hear varying qualities of movement.

The attempt here and now is to make your listening a conscious process, not merely the lapping of musical waves on placid ear drums.

Now listen to these same eight measures by Haydn one bar at a time. Do you hear that each of the last four measures "does" more than any of the first four? Just such differences in musical motion are what you are to listen for in the rest of the examples.

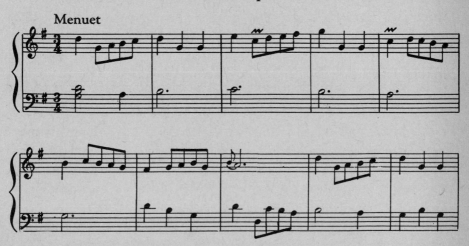

Molto allegro

MOZART

The rapidity of movement does not depend on nor does it correlate with, the numbers of notes of small values. Listen to the following example from Chopin.

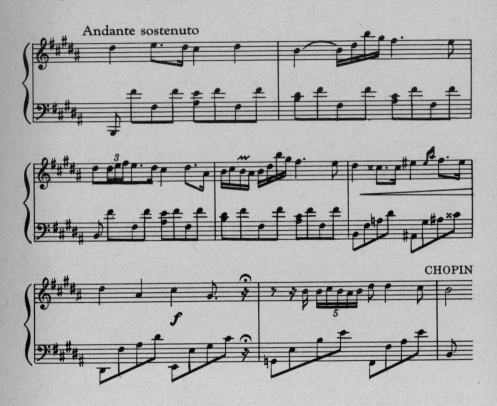

The sixteenth note figures in measures two, four, and seven are ornamentations. Do you hear that the figures

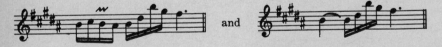

are essentially the same? Measures five and six move more directly and pointedly without having any clusters of sixteenth notes.

In the five examples thus far, each has a certain amount of rhythmic variety. The different aspects of musical motion appear as well in compositions that have a regular steady rhythm. Listen to the Bach chorale below. Though the continuity is motor-like in its regularity, there is variety in the movement.

BACH

Our problem in analysis will be to understand the structure of musical motion in one-voice compositions, namely, melodies. Now that you are able to read, hear, and manipulate basic elements of musical craft, you must try to understand how these are used in the artful expression of musical ideas.

# Section 17.

====

### Practice

Your home practice will now be left entirely up to you, since you know best what your weaknesses are.

For the most part there will have to be continued and concentrated work in intervals. You can invent exercises similar to the ones we have given, other than those using chords. Review and practice the preceding work and expand it at the points you deem necessary.

This practice combined with the preparation of sight singing melodies and a review of rhythm exercises will carry you through the remaining sections.

## Dictation

*Absolute intervals*

*Intervals in Eb major*

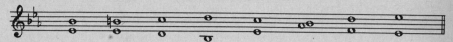

*Intervals in B minor*

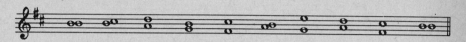

*Melodies*

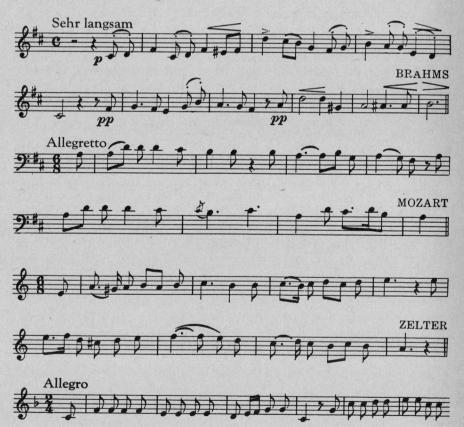

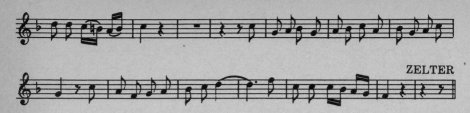

ZELTER

## Intervals

### The Major 2d; the minor 2d

The Major 2d appears in the major and minor scales between the following scale degrees:

The minor 2d appears in the major and minor scales between the following scale degrees:

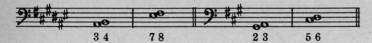

### Drill

Sing a Major 2d below each of the lowest tones of the following chords:

Sing a minor 2d above each of the top tones of the following chords:

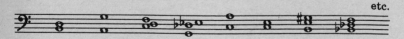

## *Sight Singing — Melodies*

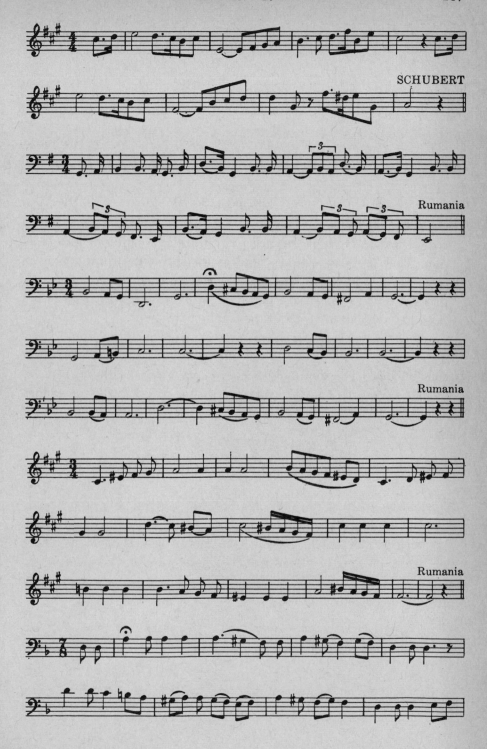

SCHUBERT

Rumania

Rumania

Rumania

## Analysis

### The use of melodies

Melodies are rarely if ever used in musical compositions merely as tunes. They are accompanied, used as themes in the construction of larger works, and employed in various other ways. Even in songs melodies are used to convey the meanings of words, and often, as in art songs, to symbolize the ideas of the text.

Melodies or melodic fragments that are used in larger forms need not be complete in structure. Their one requisite is that they have characteristic ideas. The shortest theme we know is that of the first movement of Beethoven's Fifth Symphony. Using only two different tones it presents a characteristic idea.

This idea consists of the skip of a 3rd and a rhythmic figure. This is not what we mean by a melody.

A melody has length, growth, climax, and resolution in its single line. It can be sung or played from beginning to end with a feeling of completeness. Such a melody is used as the theme of the second movement of the Beethoven Fifth.

This movement uses the many characteristic elements in the theme to build a set of variations.

## Concept of space

Musical compositions have certain similarities to paintings. The painter must decide how large or small a canvas he is going to use. The physical limits of the canvas are the physical limits of the painting. A musical composition also sets a canvas within which it works. This canvas is both of emotional and tonal size. The composer selects the few emotional qualities he wishes to express, and develops them. He does not try to run the gamut of feelings, because this leads only to chaos. The tonal space is also defined. Often we can tell certain of its limits soon after the composition begins. We can tell if the composition is tonal, if it is major or minor, if it is fast or slow, lyrical or angular, and so on. If a composition is written for a group of instruments or voices of different color, the tonal space may also include a color factor. For example, the announcement of a theme in octaves by a flute and cello sets up a wide range of color in addition to the other characteristic elements of the theme itself.

Let us turn now to folk songs in which all these extra factors are at a minimum. One voice sings the melody; there is only one color. The tunes may be performed without accompaniment, so that we are dealing with complete compositions in one voice line.

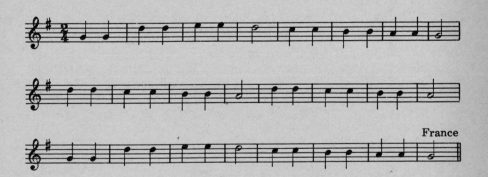

France

This melody moves in three phrases each of eight measures in length. Within each phrase there is also a smaller division into four-measure groups.

The opening measures define the space within which the melody moves. This space is a Perfect 5th.

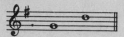

The outline of the space is made complete by the use of the neighboring tone, E. The outline of action in the first four measures is:

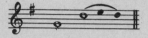

The second part of the phrase fills in this space.

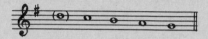

Here we see two kinds of musical movement — space-outlining and space-filling movement.

The second phrase again fills in the space, but incompletely.

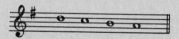

This incompleteness, ending on the second degree of G major, demands resolution. A tension is set up by the second phrase that makes the final movement down to the G imperative. Even this is held off until the space is outlined once more, and, finally, in the last four measures the melodic motion is completed. The climax of the melody comes when the space is outlined for the second time, and the final resolution of the melody must result.

Here are a few more melodies that use similar structures. Listen to them; outline the phrases; listen to hear the points to which the movement passes; then abstract the analysis. Remember, you can only

understand and analyze exactly what you hear! After hearing you will
be able to understand what unifies the structure into a complete
composition.

# Section 18.

Section 18 covers the following:

Dictation
    Absolute intervals
    Intervals in G minor
    Intervals in E major
    Melodies
Sight singing: melodies
Intervals
    The Major 7th; the minor 7th
Analysis

## Dictation

### Absolute intervals

### Intervals in G minor

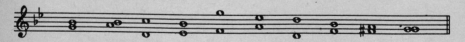

### Intervals in E major

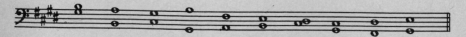

*Melodies*

## Sight Singing — Melodies

Italy

SCHUMANN

Slowly

*mf*

*f*

Scotland

Sweden

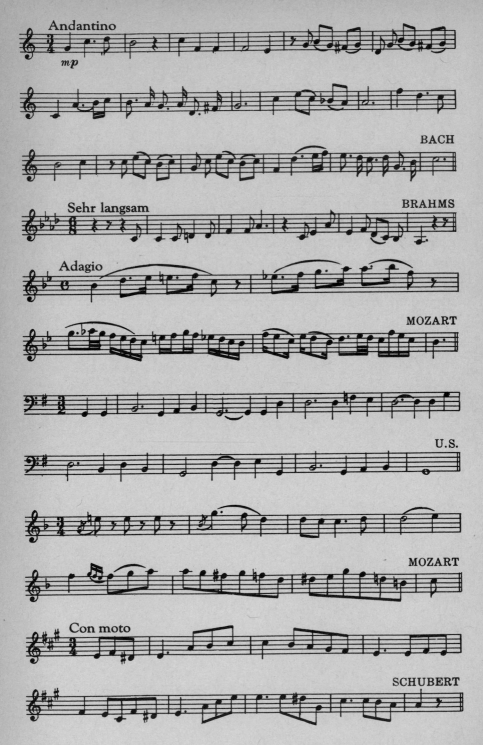

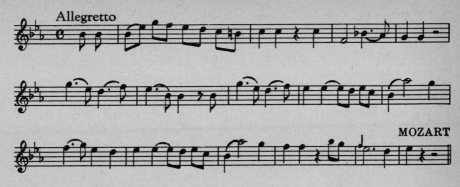

*Intervals*

### The Major 7th; the minor 7th

The Major 7th appears in the major and minor scales between the following scale degrees:

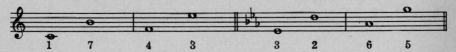

The minor 7th appears in the major and minor scales between the following scale degrees:

### Drill

Sing a Major 7th above each of the top tones of the following chords:

Sing a Major 7th below each of the lowest tones of the following chords:

Sing a minor 7th above and below each of the following tones:

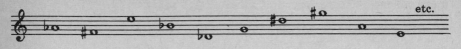

## Analysis

There are many different possibilities for extending and creating musical movement. Thus far we have seen only a few of the simplest techniques. Having witnessed the techniques of space-outlining and space-filling movements, we shall go on.

Germany

This melody consists of four phrases. Unlike the melodies already analyzed, this one devotes more time to creating and developing the outlines of space than to filling them in.

Phrase 1:

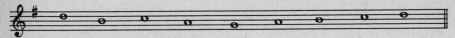

The first two measures indicate a simple ornamentation of the scale passage down from D to G.

Phrase 2:

Here the line from G up to D is incomplete; it is outlined by the tonic chord. The slight variation from the original phrase does not change the essential meaning. It tends to emphasize the D by approaching it in another way.

Phrase 3:

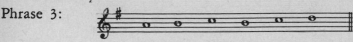

The third phrase develops the movement upwards to the limits of the musical space. The movement is in two sequences.

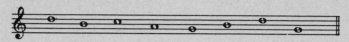

Phrase 4:

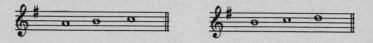

Like the opening, the downward line filling in the space comes first, and the upward movement last. Here we have had a melody that consistently resolves from the dominant to the tonic and then restates the space of a 5th. Tension is established by the reiteration and development of the upward movement outlining the canvas.

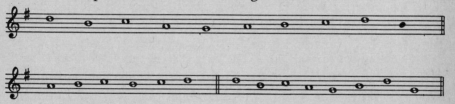

There are no set patterns in music. No law "must" or can be followed in the composition of even a simple melody. We can attempt to hear some of the basic movement principles, but each composition is a life unto itself and must be studied separately if we are to understand the broad outlines of the motion as well as the subtleties of expression.

Most of the examples so far have evidenced movement that is quite direct. For example, in moving within the space of a fifth, direct scale lines are used.

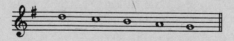

In the melody above we hear simple variations on this directness.

Instead of

we had

Instead of 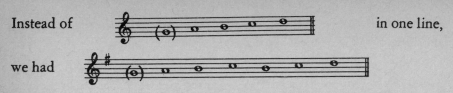 in one line,

we had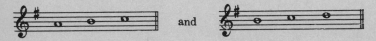

in which there are two parts

 and

Movement can be direct or indirect. The clearest form of direct move-ment is the stepwise (scale) passage. Indirect movement generally in-volves the use of ornaments, in the form of neighboring tones, other ornamental figures, or chordal ornaments.

SCHUMANN

This melody is in two parts. The first creates the space F to C, and uses an ornamental figure to emphasize the C. The second part moves irresistibly down from C to F, but punctuates each point of movement with an ornamental figure.

The larger the composition the more use is made of indirect move-ment, for in the expression of larger ideas one attempts to give a round-ed picture through varied approaches to the subject matter. In longer works the techniques of ornamentation, modulation, tone coloration, and so on tend to be used more fully.

Analyze the following melodies:

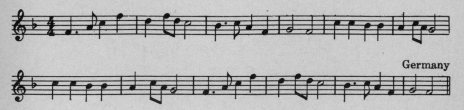

Germany

U.S.

Germany

etc.

# Section 19.

### Dictation

*Absolute intervals*

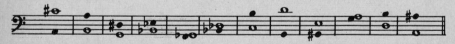

*Intervals in F minor*

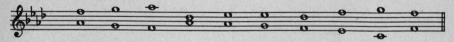

*Intervals in F# major*

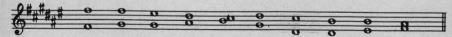

*Melodies*

*Intervals*

### The augmented 4th and diminished 5th

The augmented 4th appears in the major and minor scales between the following scale degrees:

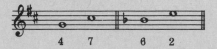

The diminished 5th appears in the major and minor scales between the following scale degrees:

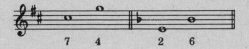

This completes the intervals as they appear in the major and minor scales. Other augmented and diminished intervals appear in mixed scales. For example, the mixed minor using the Major or raised leading tone creates an augmented 2nd between the 6th and 7th scale degrees.

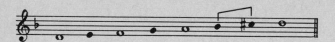

We shall not list these new interval relationships that result from mixing scales, but you will meet them and recognize them in compositions.

### Analysis

We have barely scratched the surface in analyzing musical motion, and yet there is little more we can do at this point. The few concepts you have learned will have to be integrated in your hearing so that it becomes "natural" to listen for and hear the direction and growth of a composition. In order to accomplish this we suggest more and more detailed listening and analysis. Don't be limited by the rather simple melodies we list for analysis; try any that appear in the book.

Our approach is halted momentarily by our meager knowledge. We cannot call upon any musical phenomena other than one-voice compositions. The relationship of harmony, orchestration, voice leading, and

so forth, to musical movement will be a real problem as you understand the more advanced techniques.

But you will have accomplished a great deal in musical understanding if you can hear movement and are able to recognize space-outlining,
space-filling, and direct and ornamental motion.

Analyze the following melodies:

FRANZ

SCHUMANN

### Transposition

Transposition refers to the act of shifting complete tone patterns to
different tone levels. A composition originally in F major can be trans-

posed down a 6th to A major, or to any other key. The relationship of
tones within the composition remains the same, but instead of revolving
around the key tone F it revolves around the new key tone.

Transposition is used most by accompanists and singers in making
songs conform to the range of the singer.

Example:

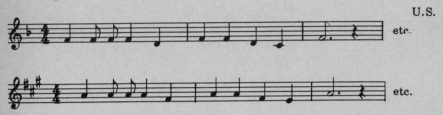

One method of transposing involves the use of different clefs. A
melody written in the treble clef can be transposed a Major 3rd higher
or a minor 6th lower by substituting the bass clef. Though one thinks
in the substitute clef, performance must be in the proper range. The
signature of the new key applies, and great care must be given to the
use of added accidentals. The pattern of the transposed melody must
be an exact duplicate of the original.

Example:

Other clefs that are useful in transposing are the C clefs.

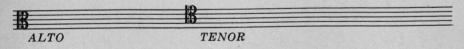

ALTO                    TENOR

The ability to handle these clefs is useful beyond the problem of transposition. The alto and tenor clefs are used regularly in orchestral
scores, and appear quite frequently in choral literature. Learn to read
these clefs in the same way you learned to read the treble and bass
clefs. Make separate cards for each note on the staff and drill.

Alto clef:

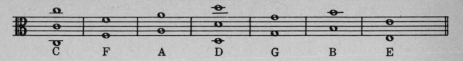

Tenor clef:

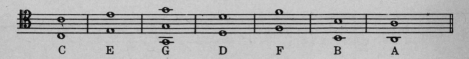

## Sight Singing — Melodies

# Section 20.

## Notes To The Teacher

Section 20 is the final section of this text. It contains only dictation exercises and sight singing melodies. The final test of musical training comes in the ability to hear and perform accurately and expressively. All that has been learned can be applied in this section. Both student and teacher are provided with adequate test material to gauge accomplishments and to determine what problems require continued study. A good part of the work should be done in class without home preparation.

### Dictation

*Absolute intervals*

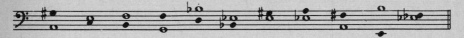

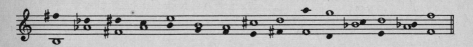

*Intervals in E minor*

*Intervals in B major*

*Intervals in F# minor*

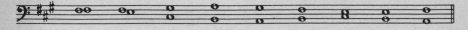

*Intervals in A♭ major*

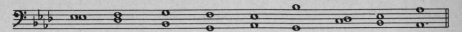

*Melodies*

BRAHMS

SCHUMANN

BACH

*Sight Singing — Melodies*

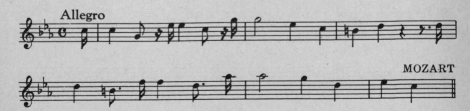

MOZART

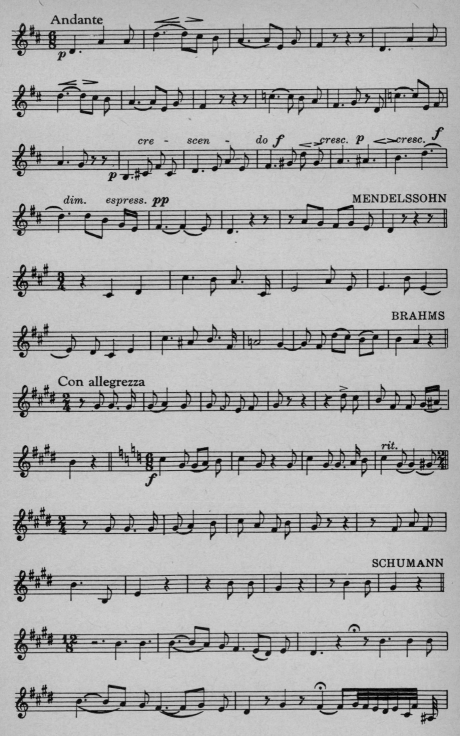

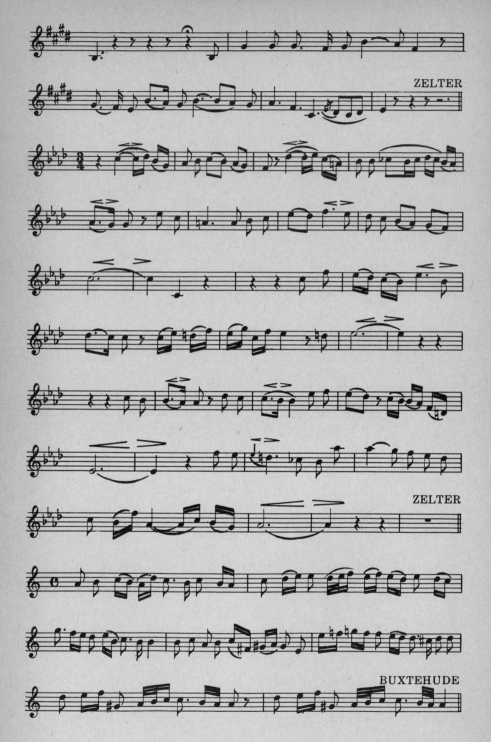

*p cantabile*

BARTOK[1]

1 Reprinted by permission of Boosey & Hawkes, Inc., New York, New York.

# Canons, Rounds, Two-
# and Three-Part Compositions

PALESTRINA

SARTORIUS

PRAETORIUS

CALDARA

AGRICOLA

TELEMANN

TELEMANN

BOYCE

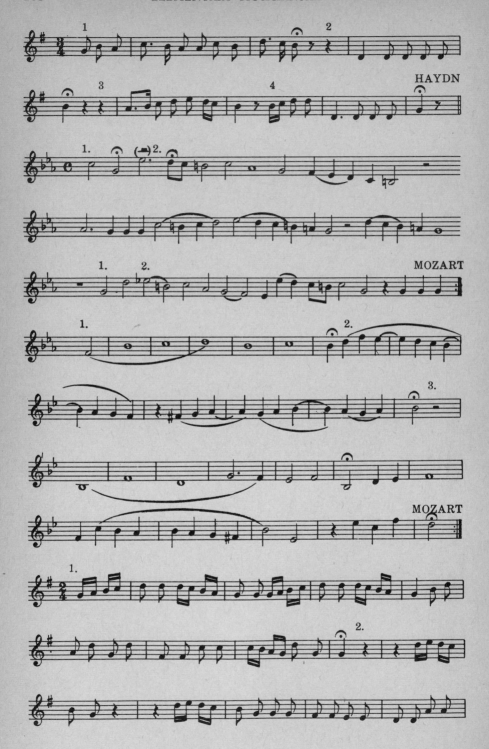

HAYDN

MOZART

MOZART

CHERUBINI

BRAHMS

PRAETORIUS

# I GO BEFORE, MY DARLING

MORLEY

I go be-fore, my dar - - - - -

I go be-fore, my

ling, I go be - fore, my dar - - - ling, I

dar - - - - ling, I go be -

go be - fore, my dar - - - ling, I

fore, my dar - - - - ling,

go be - fore, my dar - ling, I go be-fore, my

I go be - fore, my dar - - - - - -

dar - - - - ling, I go be -

ling, I be - fore, my dar - - ling, I

ly.  There  we  will  to  ge - ther,  Sweet - ly  kiss each

ly.         There  we   will  to - ge - ther,   Sweet ly

o  -  ther,   And   like  two  wan  -  tons

kiss each  o - ther,  And   like  two  wan  -  tons   Dal - ly dal - ly

Dal - ly  dal - ly   dal - ly dal - ly dal  -  ly   dal - ly

- dal - ly  dal - ly   dal - ly dal - ly dal  -  ly

dal - ly dal - ly dal  -  ly  dal  -  ly  dal - ly dal - ly dal  -  ly.

dal - ly dal - ly dal - ly  dal  -  ly dal - ly  dal - ly dal - ly dal  -  ly.

## SWEET NYMPH, COME TO THY LOVER

MORLEY

Night-in-gale with wan - - - ton with wan-ton

Where the sweet Night-in-gale with wan - ton with

glos - - es, hark her love too dis-clos - -

wan ton glos - es, hark her love too dis -

- 'es too dis-clos - es, Hark her love too dis -

clos - - - es, Hark her love too dis-clos-es

clos-es too dis-clos - - - es. Where the sweet es.

too dis-clos - - - - es. es.

## GO YE, MY CANZONETS

MORLEY

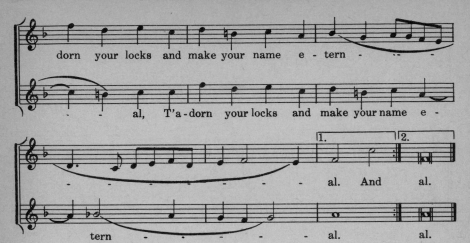

dorn your locks and make your name e - tern - - -

- - al, T'a-dorn your locks and make your name e -

- - - - - - al. And al.

tern - - - - al. al.

# WHEN LO, BY BREAK OF MORNING

MORLEY

lets and ____ Cow - slips plen - ty, The

Vi - o-lets and Cow-slips plen - ty, The birds en -

birds en-am-our'd the birds en-am-our'd sing and

am-our'd the birds en-am-our'd sing and praise my

praise my Flo - ra, Lo here a new Au - ro -

Flo - ra, Lo here a new Au -

ra. Lo here a new Au - ro - ra. Lo here a

ro - ra. Lo here a new Au - ro - ra.

new Au - ro - ra. The ra.

Lo here a new Au - ro - ra. The birds en ra.

## ALLELUIA. CONFITEMINI DOMINO

BYRD

# DREIFACH IST DER SCHRITT DER ZEIT

SCHUBERT

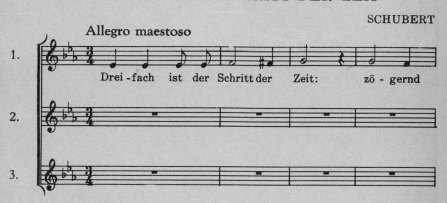

Allegro maestoso

1. Drei-fach ist der Schritt der Zeit: zö - gernd

2.

3.

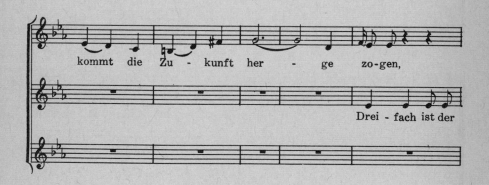

kommt die Zu - kunft her - ge zo-gen,

Drei - fach ist der

pfeil - schnell ist das Jetzt ent flo-gen,

Schritt der Zeit: zö - gernd

# SANCTUS

BYRD

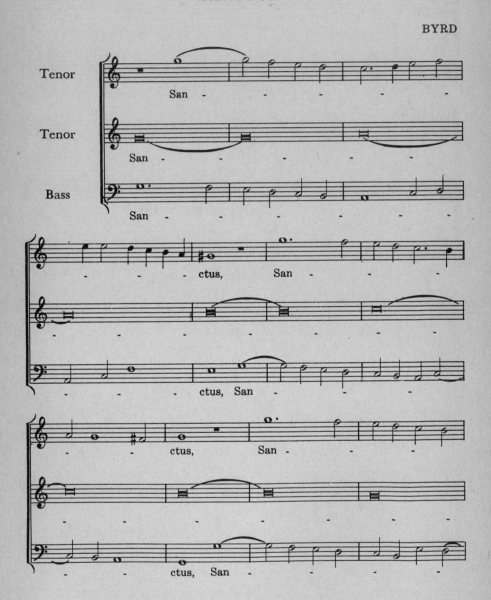

## LIEBE SÄUSELN DIE BLÄTTER

SCHUBERT

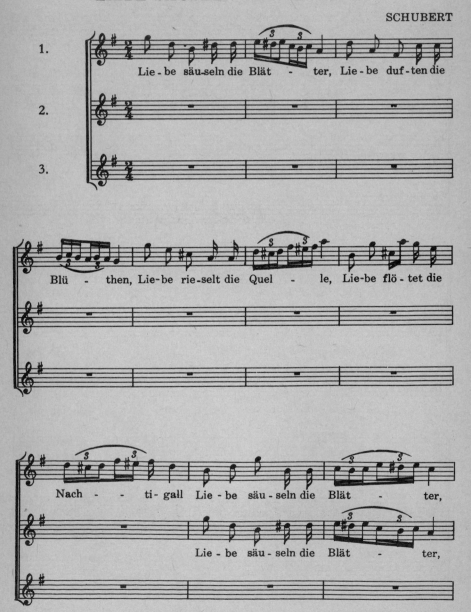

1. Lie - be säu-seln die Blät - ter, Lie - be duf - ten die

Blü - then, Lie - be rie-selt die Quel - le, Lie - be flö - tet die

Nach - ti - gall Lie - be säu - seln die Blät - ter,

Lie - be säu - seln die Blät - ter,

Lie - be duf ten - die Blü - then, Lie - be rie - selt die

Lie - be duf ten - die Blü - then, Lie - be rie - selt die

Quel - - le, Lie - be flö tettet die Nach - ti gall.

Quel - - le, Lie - be flö tettet die Nach - ti gall.

Lie - be säu - seln die Blät - ter, Lie - be

Lie - be säu - seln die Blät - ter, Lie - be duf - ten die

Lie - be säu - seln die Blät - ter, Lie - be duf - ten die

duf - ten die Blü - then, Lie - be rie - selt die Quel -

Blü - then, Lie - be rie - selt die Quel - le,

Blü - then, Lie - be rie - selt die Quel - le,

Lie - be duf - ten die Blü - then, Lie - be rie - selt die

Lie - be duf - ten die Blü - then, Lie - be rie - selt die

ter, Lie - be duf - ten die Blü - then, Lie - be

Quel - le, Lie - be flö - tet die Nach - ti - gall.

Quel - le, Lie - be flö - tet die Nach - ti - gall.

rie - selt die Quel - le, Lie - be flö - tet die Nach - ti - gall.

# DESSEN FAHNE DONNERSTURME WALLTE.

SCHUBERT

# TRINKLIED IM MAI.

SCHUBERT

freu'n! Die Win - de ver - stum - men und ath - men noch
Tisch. Be - krän - zet die Ton - nen und za - pfet mir

Mai. Er träuft auf die Blü - then sein Roth und sein
Klang; giebt Mäd - chen und Kna - ben ein Min - ne - ge -

Mai's! Es grü - ne die Lau - be die Küs - se ver -
seh'n! Ihr la - chen-den Lüf - te, bleibt hei - ter und

kaum, die Bien - lein um - sum - men den blü - hen - den
Wein! Der Mai ist be - gon - nen, wir müs - sen uns

Weiss, die Vö - ge - lein brü - ten im Schat - ten des
fühl, und herr - li - che Ga - ben zum Kuss und zum

schliesst! Es wach - se die Trau - be, der Nek - tar ent -
hell! Ihr Blü - then voll Düf - te, ver - weht nicht so

Baum. Die Win - de ver - stum - men und ath - men noch
freu'n! Be - krän - zet die Ton - nen und za - pfet mir

Mai's. Er träuft auf die Blü - then sein Roth und sein
Spiel; giebt Mäd chen und Kna - ben ein Min - ne - ge

fliesst! Es grü - ne die Lau - be die Küs - se ver -
schnell! Ihr la - chen den Lüf - te, bleibt hei - ter und

kaum, die Bien - lein um - sum - men den blü - hen - den Baum.
Wein! Der Mai ist be gon - nen, wir müs - sen uns freu'n!

Weiss, die Vö - ge - lein brü - ten im Schat - ten des Mai's.
fühl, und herr - li - che Ga - ben zum Kuss und zum Spiel.

schliesst! Es wach - se die Trau - be, der Nek - tar ent - fliesst!
hell! Ihr Blü - then voll Düf - te, ver weht nicht so schnell!

# VERSCHWUNDEN SIND DIE SCHMERZEN.

SCHUBERT.

Ver - schwun-den sind die Schmer - zen, weil aus bek-lemm-ten Her - zen kein Seuf - zer wi - der halt; drum ju - belt hoch, ihr Deut - sche, denn die ver-ruch-te Peit - sche hat end - lich aus ge-

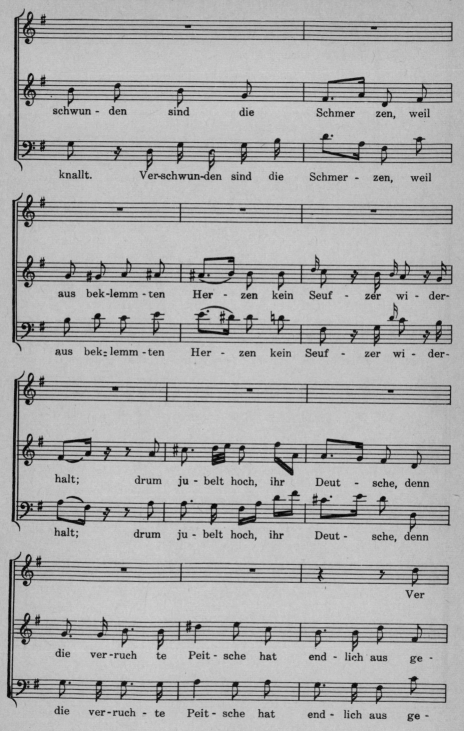

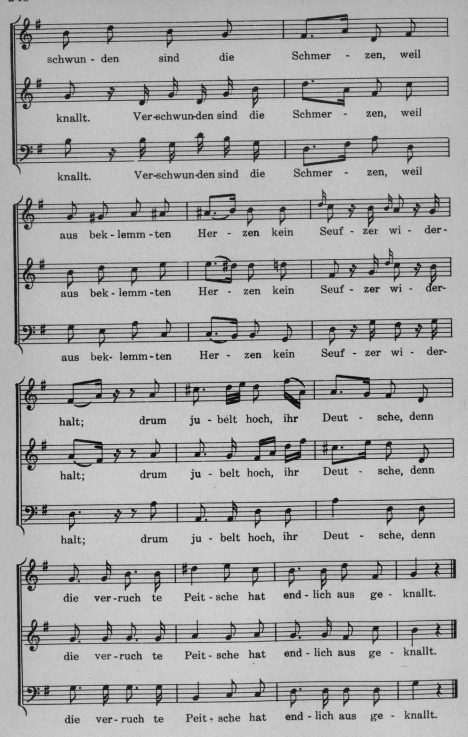